I0617259

AMERICA'S CIGAR STORY

*The History, Politics, and Legacy of Cigars from
1762 to the Modern Era*

The definitive narrative history of cigars in American life.

Sebastian Saviano

THE AMERICAN CIGAR PRESS

America's Cigar Story
The History, Politics, and Legacy of Cigars from 1762 to the Modern Era

© 2025 **Sebastian Saviano**
All rights reserved. No part of this book may be reproduced, stored in a retrieval system, or transmitted in any form or by any means—electronic, mechanical, photocopying, recording, or otherwise—without prior written permission from the publisher, except for brief quotations in critical reviews or articles.

Published by
The American Cigar Press
An imprint of Deriva Publishing

ISBN 979-8-9985117-9-0 (paperback)
ISBN 979-8-218-59811-2 (hardcover)
ISBN 979-8-9985117-8-3 (ebook)

LCCN: 2025934609

First printing, March 2025
Second printing, with corrections, May 2026

For inquiries or permissions, visit www.DerivaPublishing.com

Printed in the United States of America and in other countries.

This book is a work of historical research. While every effort has been made to ensure accuracy, the author and publisher assume no responsibility for errors, omissions, or any consequences arising from its use.

The American Cigar Series
Volume 1 of a four-volume nonfiction series exploring the cultural, political, and sensory history of cigars in American life:
Vol. 1 — *America's Cigar Story*
Vol. 2 — *Smoke & Oak*
Vol. 3 — *The American Puro*
Vol. 4 — *Cigar America*

To the craftsmen and immigrant workers
who transformed adversity into artistry—
those whose hands and stories
have shaped more than tobacco,
but a moment of reflection,
a connection to history.
May their legacy live on through these pages.

Uncle Sam Approved.

Before You Light That Cigar...

For over 250 years, cigars have shaped American history, industry, and culture—from the colonial tobacco fields to the cigar lounges of the Gilded Age, where they served as symbols of power, battlefield comforts, and quiet indulgences for workers and elites alike.

Yet most accounts focus on Cuban cigars, public-health debates, or the cigarette wars, leaving the larger American cigar story untold. This book fills that gap, tracing the rise of the American cigar industry, the labor struggles of Black and immigrant workers, and the economic forces that shaped its production and trade.

My passion for cigars and American history inspired this work. From Ybor City's bustling factories to the "smoke-filled rooms" of political power, cigars have left their mark on American life. Coming to this subject as a historian rather than a cigar industry insider, I've set out to provide a well-researched yet engaging account—one that bridges rigorous scholarship with storytelling that brings history to life.

Our journey begins in 1762 when Lt. Col. Israel Putnam brought Cuban cigars and seeds back from Havana—a small act that would seed an industry. It follows the industry's golden age in New York, Pennsylvania, and Florida, explores the Cuban Embargo's lasting impact, and examines how Nicaragua, the Dominican Republic, and Honduras emerged as new cigar powerhouses. The unexpected resurgence of premium cigars in the 1990s—fueled by celebrity culture, brands, and *Cigar Aficionado*—shows their enduring place in American life.

America's cigar story is one of craftsmanship, resilience, and tradition. Whether you're an aficionado, a historian, or simply curious about cigars' role in American culture, I invite you to explore this rich and complex history.

And my invitation comes with a promise: the reading will be enjoyable. So, sit back and light up that stogie.

Sebastian Saviano
March 2025

TABLE OF CONTENTS

INTRODUCTION

More Than Just a Smoke

Israel Putnam came back from Havana in 1762 with donkey loads of Cuban cigars and a packet of seeds | He had no idea what he had started. Two and a half centuries later, the cigar he carried home has shown up at nearly every turn in American life — at the surrender at Appomattox, in the smoke-filled rooms where presidents got picked, in the immigrant factories of Ybor City, in the Oval Office the night before Kennedy signed the Cuban embargo, and in the cigar lounges where the 1990s boom decided what wealth was supposed to look like.

From the back rooms where political deals shaped the nation to the battlefields where soldiers clung to cigars as a brief solace amid chaos, these hand-rolled artifacts have played an outsized role in shaping American culture. They were in the hands of the industrialists who transformed the economy, the presidents who wielded global influence, and the workers whose craftsmanship and labor built an industry that shaped American commerce and influenced cigar culture worldwide.

While Havana cigars have long been revered, America played a critical—if often overlooked—role in the cultivation, production, and commercialization of cigars. From Connecticut's famed tobacco fields to Tampa's cigar factories, from the labor struggles of cigar workers to the glamour of Hollywood's golden age, the American cigar story is one of innovation, resilience, and cultural significance.

Why This Book? Why Now?

Despite the cigar's prominence in American history, its story remains largely untold. *America's Cigar Story* is an exploration of how cigars shaped and were shaped by business, politics, war, and social culture. This book spans centuries, tracing the rise of cigars in colonial America beginning in 1762, their role in the War of 1812 and the Civil War, the golden age of cigar factories, the 1962 Cuban Embargo, the 1990s cigar boom, and the modern boutique revival.

In telling this story, we will answer key questions, such as:

- How did cigars evolve from a European import to an American cultural staple?
- What role did cigars play in early American political and economic development?
- How did the rise and fall of American cigar factories reflect broader societal changes?
- What was the real impact of the Cuban Embargo, and how did the cigar industry adapt?
- Why did cigars make a comeback in the 1990s, and what does the future of American cigar culture look like?

What This Book Covers

Each chapter of this book explores a different era of America's cigar legacy, showing how cigars have been shaped by historical forces—from colonial trade and wartime consumption to industrial innovation and cultural renaissance.

Chapter 1: The Foundations of American Cigar Culture
Cigars arrived in America as an imported luxury but quickly became a symbol of economic and cultural identity. This chapter explores the colonial tobacco economy, the role of Cuban cigars in early America, and how wars—from the War of 1812 to the Civil War—cemented cigars as part of American life.

Chapter 2: The Rise of the American Cigar Industry
The Industrial Revolution transformed cigar-making from an artisan craft to a mass-market industry. As immigration surged, cigar factories in New York, Philadelphia, and Tampa became centers of economic opportunity—but also of labor struggles and political tensions.

Chapter 3: Smoke-Filled Rooms & The Politics of Power
The late 19th and early 20th centuries saw cigars become a symbol of power, influence, and wealth. From Gilded Age tycoons to presidents wielding cigars in backroom political deals, this chapter explores how cigars became deeply intertwined with American politics and business culture.

Chapter 4: The Cuban Embargo: A Defining Disruption
The 1962 Cuban Embargo forever altered the cigar industry. This chapter explores how the Cold War and Cuba's alignment with the Soviet Union led to the sudden disappearance of Cuban cigars from the U.S. market—against the backdrop of John F. Kennedy's last-minute cigar stockpile—forcing the industry to reinvent itself with new production hubs in Nicaragua, Honduras, and the Dominican Republic.

Chapter 5: The 1990s Cigar Revival
By the late 20th century, cigars had faded from mainstream American culture. Then came an unexpected revival, fueled by celebrity culture, Wall Street wealth, and *Cigar Aficionado* magazine. This chapter examines the cigar boom of the 1990s and how it reshaped the market—setting the stage for today's cigar renaissance.

Chapter 6: The Boutique Cigar Renaissance
The 21st century ushered in a new era of craftsmanship, as boutique brands began challenging industry giants. This chapter explores how small-batch manufacturers, experimental blending, and the resurgence of American-grown tobacco are reshaping the cigar world today.

Chapter 7: The Future of the Cigar Industry
As cigars face increasing government regulations, changing consumer habits, and shifting global markets, their future remains uncertain. This final chapter examines what lies ahead for cigars in the United States, exploring

debates over Food and Drug Administration (FDA) oversight, taxation, international trade, and the rise of digital cigar communities.

The Enduring Allure of the Cigar

Perhaps more than any other tobacco product, cigars have resisted mass-market commodification. Unlike cigarettes, which became a disposable convenience, cigars have remained a deliberate indulgence, requiring time, patience, and appreciation. Their enduring appeal lies not just in the tobacco itself, but in the ritual—the cutting, the lighting, the slow, contemplative burn.

It is a ritual that has survived economic depressions, war, shifting social norms, and government regulations. Even today, in a world of fast-paced consumer culture, cigar lounges remain a place where time slows down.

Welcome to *America's Cigar Story*—a journey through smoke, craft, and history.

CHAPTER 1

The Foundations of
American Cigar Culture

From Colonies to Civil War [1] | The story of early American history is one of extraordinary transformation. Between 1607 and 1865, the North American colonies evolved from scattered European settlements into a unified republic—one that would soon be tested by war. What began as an economic outpost for European imperial powers became a nation shaped by the ideals of self-governance, economic expansion, and territorial ambition. Yet, as the country grew in power and influence, deep political and economic divisions threatened to tear it apart.

The 18th century saw the American colonies break away from British rule in a radical experiment in self-governance. The American Revolution (1775–1783) was not just a military conflict but a declaration that democracy could challenge existing global power structures. Economically, the colonies thrived on agriculture and transatlantic trade, exporting

---

[1] *A Note Moving Forward: America's cigar story is inseparable from the nation's political, economic, and cultural evolution. In many ways, it mirrors its history. To provide context, each chapter begins with a 'historical context' section, linking cigar industry developments to broader American events.*

tobacco, rice, indigo, and cotton to European markets. This prosperity, however, depended on an exploitative labor system—indentured servitude and slavery—both of which would sow the seeds of future conflict.

As the 19th century progressed, the country expanded rapidly. The Louisiana Purchase (1803) and subsequent territorial acquisitions fueled the ideology of Manifest Destiny, reinforcing America's belief in its right to expand westward. However, this territorial growth intensified political tensions between the North and South, particularly regarding slavery's role in the economy. The War of 1812 (1812–1815) further defined the nation's identity, solidifying U.S. sovereignty and opening new trade opportunities.

By the mid-1800s, the North had developed a powerful industrial economy, while the South remained largely agrarian and dependent on enslaved labor. These economic and moral divides culminated in the Civil War (1861–1865), the most profound crisis in U.S. history. The war ultimately led to the abolition of slavery (13th Amendment, 1865) and redefined citizenship, paving the way for Reconstruction. Additionally, the industrial mobilization required during the war laid the groundwork for the United States' emergence as a global economic power in the following decades.

Throughout these years of transformation, America was not only building a nation—it was also shaping its cultural identity. Cigars, once a rare imported luxury, began to take root in American society during this period. The next section explores how this shift occurred, tracing the early roots of cigar culture from the colonial era through the Civil War and the key regions that shaped American cigar-making.

The Evolution of America and the Birth of Cigar Culture

Long before cigars became a symbol of power and refinement in America, tobacco had already shaped the country's economy, politics, and daily life. In the early American colonies, tobacco was more than a mere cash crop— it was a lifeline, a currency, and a commodity that connected the New World to Europe and the Caribbean. Farmers, merchants, and even the

Founding Fathers depended on its trade to sustain their wealth and ambitions. Yet, while tobacco cultivation was firmly entrenched in American society by the 17th century, the cigar as we know it was still a rarity. It would take another century before cigars evolved from a mostly imported indulgence into a staple of American culture.

This chapter explores that transformation, tracing the earliest roots of American cigar culture from its introduction in the 18th century to its rising popularity among soldiers, industrialists, and statesmen in the 19th. It also examines the critical role played by key tobacco-growing regions—such as Pennsylvania and Connecticut—whose fertile lands shaped the future of American cigar-making.

The Role of Tobacco in the Colonial Economy

Tobacco transformed the struggling American colonies into an economic powerhouse. In the Chesapeake region of Virginia and Maryland, this "golden leaf" became more than a crop—it was the foundation of colonial society, serving as both commodity and currency.

The story begins with John Rolfe's successful tobacco cultivation in Jamestown in 1612. His first shipment to England in 1614 marked the beginning of a commercial revolution in the colonies. By 1622, Virginia's tobacco exports reached 60,000 pounds; by 1639, they surged to 1.5 million pounds. At the century's end, Britain was importing over 20 million pounds annually from its American colonies, fundamentally reshaping the colonial economy.

Tobacco's influence extended far beyond agriculture. Colonial governments began setting fixed rates for goods and services in pounds of tobacco, even requiring it for tax payments and official salaries. The crop's demands led to the widespread use of indentured servants and enslaved labor, making tobacco a primary driver of the transatlantic slave trade in North America.

The tobacco trade also shaped colonial infrastructure. Strategic ports— Norfolk, Baltimore, and Charleston—grew into economic powerhouses, their locations ideal for connecting inland plantations to transatlantic trade routes. A network of tobacco warehouses and inspection stations emerged, ensuring quality control and regulated exports.

Yet this prosperity came with volatility. Tobacco prices fluctuated wildly based on European demand and British trade restrictions. The Navigation Acts of the 17th century, requiring all colonial tobacco to be shipped exclusively to England, created deep-seated frustrations among American planters. These economic tensions would later contribute to the growing rift between the colonies and the British Crown—one of many factors that would ultimately spark the American Revolution.

As colonial America grew from a collection of struggling settlements into a network of prosperous colonies, the way Americans consumed their precious tobacco underwent an equally significant transformation. While tobacco had already established itself as the economic backbone of colonial society, the shift from pipes to cigars marked a crucial evolution in American cultural independence.

The early colonial period was dominated by clay pipes, most imported from England alongside other manufactured goods. These pipes, mass-produced in cities like Bristol and London, symbolized the colonies' commercial and cultural ties to Britain. Even as colonial craftsmen developed their own pipe-making traditions, using local materials and designs, the basic form remained rooted in European customs.

However, the same merchant ships that carried Virginia and Maryland tobacco to European markets began returning from Seville—the birthplace of modern cigar manufacturing—carrying something new: expertly hand-rolled cigars. These tobacco products, first perfected in the Royal Tobacco Factory of Seville in the early 1700s, represented a dramatic departure from British smoking traditions. As colonial traders increased their connections with Spanish territories, particularly in response to restrictive British trade policies, they encountered a sophisticated cigar culture that would soon captivate American smokers.

The practical advantages of cigars over pipes became immediately apparent. While pipes required constant maintenance and were prone to breakage, cigars offered a self-contained, portable smoking experience ideally suited to America's increasingly mobile society. Merchants, sailors, and travelers found they could easily carry a supply of cigars for their journeys, and soldiers discovered them to be far more convenient during military campaigns.

By the 1750s, the first attempts at American cigar-making emerged in colonial port cities, often involving craftsmen who had learned their trade from Spanish or Cuban artisans. While most cigars were still imported during this period, these early manufacturers began adapting traditional techniques to local tobacco varieties. The practice gradually spread inland, reaching agricultural regions like Lancaster County, where farmers began experimenting with tobacco varieties specifically suited for cigar production.

This transformation in tobacco consumption foreshadowed America's broader journey toward independence. Just as colonial merchants sought trade relationships beyond Britain, American smokers began embracing alternatives to British-style pipe tobacco. Cigars became symbols of sophistication and worldliness, representing a break from colonial traditions and the emergence of a new American cultural identity—one that would soon express itself in revolution.

Lancaster County and Pennsylvania's Role in Cigar History

Beyond Virginia and Maryland, Pennsylvania—particularly Lancaster County—emerged as a significant tobacco-growing region in the mid-19th century. The area became known for its high-quality Pennsylvania Broadleaf tobacco, which was first introduced around 1828 and gained prominence in the 1840s. Farmers developed this variety for its dark, rich flavor and durability, making it particularly favored for use as a cigar wrapper.

The Amish and Mennonite communities of Lancaster County played an essential role in this industry, growing and harvesting tobacco for generations. By the 19th century, Amish farmers were producing large quantities of tobacco, supplying it to cigar manufacturers in Pennsylvania and beyond. Their traditional farming techniques and resistance to mechanization meant that Amish-grown tobacco was often regarded as superior due to its hand-tended quality.

One of the most significant landmarks in Lancaster's cigar history is Demuth's Tobacco Shop, established in 1770 by Christopher Demuth and operated by six generations of the Demuth family until its closure in 2010 — at the time, the oldest tobacco shop in the United States. Today the storefront at 114 East King Street stands as a historical landmark, opened occasionally for special events by the Demuth Foundation, a testament to Lancaster's long-standing influence in the American cigar trade.

Despite industrialization, Lancaster County and its Amish tobacco farmers remain critical contributors to Pennsylvania's cigar tobacco industry, supplying premium leaf to domestic and international markets. Their continued presence underscores the deep historical ties between tobacco, American agriculture, and cigar culture.

Lt. Col. Putnam and the Introduction of Cuban Cigars (1762)

One of the most significant moments in early American cigar history occurred in 1762 when then-Lt. Colonel Israel Putnam, a veteran of the British campaign against Spain in the Caribbean during the Seven Years' War, returned to Connecticut with a supply of Havana cigars and Cuban tobacco seeds. This event is widely credited with the introduction of Cuban-style cigars to the American colonies.[2]

---

[2] Israel Putnam's introduction of Cuban cigars in 1762 represents a pivotal moment in early American tobacco history, documented in multiple historical accounts of colonial agricultural practices and trade networks.

Putnam, already a prominent figure in colonial New England, is believed to have distributed Cuban cigars among the local gentry, igniting a newfound appreciation for the product. More significantly, the Cuban tobacco seeds he brought back were cultivated in the Connecticut River Valley, which would later become one of the most important cigar tobacco-producing regions in the world. Over time, Connecticut-grown wrapper leaf became known for its high quality and adaptability, giving rise to what is now known as Connecticut Shade and Connecticut Broadleaf tobacco—two varieties that remain integral to premium cigar production today.

Maj. Gen. Israel Putnam. Published by D.C. Fabronius, Boston, 1864.

Following Putnam's introduction of Cuban cigars, New England and other colonial markets saw a growing demand for handmade cigars, which were initially imported but later manufactured domestically in small workshops. By the turn of the 19th century, American cigar production was well underway, laying the foundation for the industry's rapid expansion.

The War of 1812 & The Spread of Cigar Smoking

The War of 1812 played a crucial role in the spread of cigar smoking across the United States. American soldiers stationed in the Caribbean and Spanish-held territories encountered cigar-smoking traditions firsthand, particularly in Cuba and the Gulf of Mexico region. Many returning soldiers brought their newfound appreciation for cigars home, fueling domestic demand.

During this period, officers and soldiers alike increasingly favored cigars over traditional pipe smoking due to their convenience and portability in battle conditions. The war also strengthened trade ties between the U.S. and the Spanish Caribbean, ensuring a steady influx of high-quality Cuban cigars into American markets. The influence of Spanish cigar-making techniques became even more pronounced, leading to the establishment of small-scale cigar production in urban centers like New Orleans, Baltimore, and New York.

As a result, cigar smoking became associated with military prestige and leadership, further embedding the habit into American culture. Political and business leaders, many of whom had military backgrounds, helped cement cigars as a status symbol, a trend that would continue into the mid-19th century.

Cigars and the American Civil War (1861–1865)

The Civil War saw an explosion in cigar smoking among soldiers in the North and South, but particularly in the Union ranks. Officers and enlisted men alike turned to cigars for a variety of reasons: as a means of relaxation, a source of comfort, and a symbol of camaraderie. Cigars were often included in care packages sent from home, and soldiers would share them with comrades during downtime between battles.

One of the most famous cigar smokers of the war was General Ulysses S. Grant, who became synonymous with cigars. After a newspaper article described him as constantly smoking during battles, admirers began sending him cigars in droves. He reportedly received thousands of cigars as gifts, cementing his image as a cigar-smoking military leader.

In the trenches and camps, cigars were often used for bartering—soldiers would trade cigars for rations, coffee, or other goods. The prominence of cigars in wartime culture solidified their place as a symbol of resilience and endurance. The war also saw the expansion of cigar production to meet growing demand, with factories in the North ramping up output to supply soldiers on the front lines.

After the war, many veterans continued their smoking habits, further integrating cigars into mainstream American culture. The post-war boom in cigar production and consumption helped set the stage for the cigar industry's dominance in the late 19th century.

The Civil War played a significant role in expanding cigar consumption across the United States, including the West. Soldiers on both sides of the conflict routinely smoked cigars in camp, during marches, and even in battle. After the war, thousands of veterans migrated westward, bringing their tobacco habits with them. Many settled in burgeoning railroad towns and cattle outposts, where cigar smoking became an enduring part of the social and economic life of the frontier.

During this period, saloons became central hubs of Western society, particularly in fast-growing towns such as Dodge City, Kansas; Virginia City, Nevada; Deadwood, South Dakota; and Tombstone, Arizona. These establishments catered to cowboys, miners, gamblers, and businessmen, offering whiskey, gambling, and, invariably, cigars. As seen in surviving advertisements from the era, saloons often stocked a range of cigars, from inexpensive locally made varieties to imported Cuban selections that signified wealth and status.

The Lost Cigar Dispatch of 1862

One of the most famous incidents involving cigars in American history occurred during the Maryland Campaign of the Civil War. In September 1862, Union soldiers discovered three cigars wrapped in a piece of paper on an abandoned Confederate campsite near Frederick, Maryland. The seemingly innocuous find turned out to be General Robert E. Lee's Special Order 191, a detailed document outlining Confederate troop movements.

The discovery of these cigars—and more importantly, the military orders wrapped around them—provided Union General George B. McClellan with an unprecedented intelligence windfall. Special Order 191, as it was officially known, revealed Lee's entire battle plan and the dangerous division of his forces ("Special Order 191: The Lost Dispatch." National

Archives Digital Collections). The orders were discovered by Union soldiers Sergeant John Bloss and Corporal Barton W. Mitchell on September 13, 1862, in a field near Frederick, Maryland.

Armed with knowledge of Lee's movements, McClellan advanced his army to confront the divided Confederate forces, leading to the Battle of Antietam on September 17, 1862—the bloodiest single-day battle in American military history. While McClellan's characteristic caution prevented him from fully exploiting this intelligence advantage, the resulting battle nevertheless halted Lee's invasion of the North. This crucial Union victory gave President Lincoln the political opportunity he had been waiting for: just five days after the battle, he issued the preliminary Emancipation Proclamation, transforming the war's fundamental purpose from preserving the Union to ending slavery.

As the Civil War reshaped America's political landscape, it also transformed the nation's relationship with cigars. Veterans returning home brought their smoking habits to every corner of the country, creating unprecedented demand for quality cigars. This new market attracted entrepreneurs like Roger G. Sullivan, who would help define American cigar manufacturing in the post-war era.

Roger G. Sullivan: Exemplifying American Craftsmanship in the 19th-Century Cigar Industry

Roger G. Sullivan's early efforts in establishing his cigar manufacturing business in Manchester, New Hampshire, during the mid to late 1800s exemplified the intersection of American craftsmanship and entrepreneurial spirit in a rapidly industrializing nation. Born in 1854 to Irish immigrant parents, Sullivan's rise mirrored the broader economic transformation of post-Civil War America, where skilled trades and localized industries flourished before large-scale mechanization dominated production.

Starting with just two employees, he built The Sullivan Cigar Company during an era when the cigar industry was booming across the Northeast, with cities like New York, Philadelphia, and Boston serving as major hubs of tobacco commerce. Unlike mass-produced cigars that emerged later with mechanization, Sullivan upheld traditional hand-rolling techniques, ensuring high-quality products that reflected the artisanal nature of American manufacturing at the time.

His decision to base his operations in Manchester—then a center of textile production and industrial growth—positioned him within a network of skilled labor and trade infrastructure essential for expansion. By introducing his now-famous ten-cent 7-20-4 cigar, Sullivan not only demonstrated a keen understanding of market accessibility but also reinforced the American ideal that hard work and innovation could transform small enterprises into major industrial players.

While entrepreneurs like Sullivan celebrated the potential of industrial growth and market expansion, the human cost of such progress often remained hidden from public view. The same networks of skilled labor and economic infrastructure that enabled Sullivan's ten-cent cigar empire also contributed to exploitative labor conditions, particularly for children. In the shadows of industrial success, a different story was unfolding—one of young hands rolling tobacco, of childhood interrupted by economic necessity, and of an emerging industrial landscape that valued productivity over human dignity.

The Invisible Workforce: Children in the Cigar Factories

In the early 20th century, the vibrant cigar industry of Ybor City concealed a stark reality behind its bustling workshops: the widespread employment of child workers. A haunting photograph by Lewis Hine, a pioneering photographer and social reformer, taken in January 1909 at the De Pedro Casellas Cigar Factory in Tampa, Florida, captures this hidden narrative with devastating clarity.

The image below reveals a young apprentice, barely in his early teens, hunched over a workbench, his small hands engaged in the intricate process of cigar rolling.

A child apprentice at the De Pedro Casellas Cigar Factory, Tampa, 1909. Photograph by Lewis Hine.

Before the implementation of comprehensive child labor laws, young children were not just occasional workers but a critical component of the cigar manufacturing ecosystem. In Ybor City, these children often worked alongside their parents, their nimble fingers and lower wage demands making them attractive to factory owners. Families facing economic hardship saw child labor as a necessary survival strategy, with children contributing significantly to household income.

The economic landscape of early 20th century Tampa was unforgiving. Immigrant families, particularly those from Cuba and Spain, found themselves in a precarious financial position. The cigar factories, while providing employment, operated on a ruthless economic model that prioritized production and profit over worker welfare. Children as young as eight or nine would spend twelve-hour days in poorly ventilated factories, their small bodies bent over tobacco leaves, their childhood sacrificed to the demands of industrial capitalism.

Lewis Hine was instrumental in exposing these labor practices. Working for the National Child Labor Committee, he used his camera as a tool of social documentation and advocacy. His photographs were not mere images but powerful testimonies that would eventually help drive legislative reforms. By humanizing the abstract concept of child labor, Hine forced middle-class America to confront the human cost of its industrial prosperity.

The cigar factories of Ybor City were microcosms of a broader national issue. They represented a complex intersection of immigration, industrial development, and economic survival. Children were not just workers but symbols of a community's resilience, their labor a testament to the immigrant experience in early 20th century America.

By 1938, the Fair Labor Standards Act would finally provide significant protections for child workers, marking a crucial turning point in American labor history. But for the children of Ybor City's cigar factories, this protection would come after years of exploitation, their childhood memories etched with the smell of tobacco and the rhythm of endless, repetitive work.

The story of Ybor City's child laborers was not an isolated phenomenon, but part of a larger narrative of industrial transformation that reshaped tobacco production across the United States. As the cigar industry evolved from local craft to national enterprise, its geographical and cultural expressions became as diverse as the country itself. While Eastern factories mechanized and Florida's workshops relied on immigrant labor, the American West was developing its own unique tobacco ecosystem—one that would challenge and complement the industrial models of the East.

Cigar Culture in the American West: Tobacco, Trade, and Tradition in the Frontier Era

The presence of cigars in the American West was deeply intertwined with the broader patterns of migration, trade, and industrial expansion that characterized the 18th and 19th centuries. Unlike the more industrialized tobacco production hubs of the Eastern United States, where large factories in New York and Pennsylvania mechanized cigar manufacturing by the late 19th century, the West retained a more diverse and localized cigar culture, shaped by Spanish colonial influence, indigenous practices, and the rapid commercial development of frontier towns.

Early Tobacco Traditions in the Spanish Southwest (1700s–Early 1800s)

The introduction of cigars to the western territories can be traced back to Spanish colonization in the 17th and 18th centuries. Spanish settlers, who had long cultivated tobacco in the Caribbean and Mexico, established missions and agricultural settlements in present-day Texas, New Mexico, Arizona, and California. These communities, connected to Mexico via the El Camino Real trade route, relied on Cuban and Mexican tobacco for cigar production, with the Spanish elite in colonial outposts favoring rolled cigars over the pipe-smoking traditions of many indigenous tribes.

At the same time, Native American communities of the Southwest had their own long-standing traditions of tobacco use. While pipes remained a primary method of consumption, evidence suggests that rolled tobacco—early forms of cigars—were used in trade and ritual ceremonies. Spanish missionaries and merchants introduced refined cigar-making techniques, which gradually spread northward, blending with local customs and practices.

Cigars and the Frontier Economy (1820s–1860s)

By the early 19th century, tobacco had become a common trade commodity in the expanding frontier economy. American fur traders and merchants, traveling along the Santa Fe Trail and Oregon Trail, carried cigars among their goods, exchanging them alongside whiskey, firearms, and other supplies at trading posts across the Plains and Rocky Mountain regions. As military outposts expanded into the West, particularly following the Indian Removal Act (1830) and the annexation of Texas (1845), cigars became a staple of army life, with officers and enlisted men alike embracing the habit.

The discovery of gold in California in 1848, followed by subsequent gold and silver rushes in Colorado (1859), Nevada (1859), and Montana (1860s), dramatically accelerated the westward expansion of cigar culture. San Francisco rapidly emerged as the commercial gateway to the Pacific, with its port receiving premium shipments of cigars from Havana, New Orleans, and Mexico *(see Endnote 1, page 174).* By the 1850s, U.S. manufacturers were producing "clear Havanas" made with Cuban leaf, retailing them at four to five times the price of domestic cigars. The city's explosive economic growth created an insatiable demand for luxury goods, with cigars becoming a symbol of sophistication among miners, investors, and the emerging upper class of the West Coast. Hand-rolled cigar businesses proliferated, particularly within San Francisco's Chinese community, further cementing the city's reputation as a hub of tobacco commerce.

While the Eastern seaboard established itself as America's primary cigar-manufacturing hub, the nation's westward expansion carried cigar culture across the continent. As veterans, merchants, and settlers pushed toward the Pacific, they brought their smoking preferences with them, creating new markets and traditions that would blend Eastern refinement with frontier practicality.

Cigar Manufacturing in the West (Late 1800s)

By the latter half of the 19th century, cigar manufacturing had taken hold in major Western cities. San Francisco emerged as a leading producer, with a thriving industry that employed thousands of workers, many of whom were Chinese immigrants who had arrived in California to work on the Transcontinental Railroad. With the completion of the railroad in 1869, tobacco shipments from the East increased, further integrating Western cities into the national cigar trade.

Beyond California, other cities such as Denver, Kansas City, and St. Louis became regional cigar hubs, supplying tobacco products to the surrounding frontier settlements. These local industries relied on skilled hand-rollers, producing cigars that were tailored to regional preferences. Unlike the mechanized factories of the Northeast, cigar production in the West remained relatively artisanal, often operated by small family-run businesses or immigrant laborers.

Cigars as Symbols of Western Identity

As cigar culture matured in the West, it became associated with some of the era's most iconic figures. Wild Bill Hickok, one of the most famous gunfighters of the Old West, was often photographed with a cigar in hand. Bat Masterson, a lawman and journalist, was known for his preference for high-quality cigars. Wyatt Earp, the legendary lawman of Tombstone, reportedly favored fine cigars imported from the East. In literature, Mark Twain, who spent several years in the West as a journalist and humorist, further cemented the image of the cigar-smoking frontiersman through his writings.

Cigars also held broader social significance. In an era when refined leisure habits were often associated with the urban elite, cigar smoking allowed frontier men to project an air of sophistication, even in rough-and-tumble environments. In gambling halls and gentlemen's clubs, cigars were an essential part of high-stakes poker games, business dealings, and political discussions.

By the close of the 19th century, cigar culture in the American West had evolved from its Spanish colonial roots into a distinct and widely embraced tradition. From the early days of trade along the El Camino Real to the thriving manufacturing hubs of San Francisco and Denver, cigars had become both a luxury item and a commonplace indulgence among settlers, soldiers, and cowboys alike. The cigar's presence in the saloons, railcars, and mining camps of the frontier reflected broader patterns of economic and cultural exchange, serving as a marker of status, masculinity, and the enduring appeal of handcrafted goods in an increasingly industrialized world.

WHAT DID THEY SMOKE?

A Connoisseur's Guide to Early American Cigars

The evolution of American cigar preferences tells its own fascinating story of the nation's development. From colonial experiments to established brands, the cigars enjoyed by historical figures and common citizens alike reflected the changing tastes and economic conditions of their times.

When Israel Putnam returned from Cuba in 1762, he brought donkey loads of Cuban cigars. These cigars, crafted in the Spanish style, would have been quite different from the machine-made products of later eras. Each one was rolled by hand using traditional Cuban methods perfected over centuries.

During the Civil War, General Ulysses S. Grant's cigar preferences became legendary. Initially a light smoker before the Battle of Fort Donelson, Grant developed a deeper appreciation for fine cigars as the war progressed. Among his personal effects was a specially crafted cigar case, hand-carved from Lookout Mountain wood by a Union soldier. In his final years, Grant showed particular loyalty to the "Las Palmas" brand, examples of which are now preserved in historical collections.

In the late 19th and early 20th centuries, Roger G. Sullivan's 7-20-4 cigars epitomized the height of American cigar craftsmanship. These handmade cigars were crafted with Havana filler tobacco and Sumatra wrappers, earning a strong reputation in New England. The brand remained a dominant force in regional cigar manufacturing for decades.

Though the Cuban Embargo of 1962–1963 disrupted access to Cuban tobacco, the company's decline began earlier as the American cigar industry shifted toward mechanization.

On the frontier, cigars became both a luxury and a necessity of social life. Frontier saloons typically sold premium cigars for 5 cents, making them an affordable indulgence for most working men. The importance of cigars in Western society was such that larger saloons maintained dedicated cigar concessions near their entrances, allowing both men and women to purchase cigars without entering the main saloon area—a careful accommodation of Victorian social sensibilities.

For the Native American tribes and early settlers of Lancaster County, Pennsylvania, tobacco was primarily used in pipes, but as cigar production grew in the region, Pennsylvania Broadleaf tobacco became prized for its burning qualities and rich flavor. The Amish farmers' dedication to traditional growing methods produced leaf particularly suited for cigar wrapper and binder, contributing to Pennsylvania's reputation for quality tobacco production.

These varied smoking traditions—from Cuban-inspired hand-rolls to mass-produced yet quality-conscious brands—demonstrate how American cigar culture evolved to embrace both Old World craftsmanship and New World innovation. The cigars smoked by our historical figures were more than mere tobacco products; they were artifacts of their time, reflecting the tastes, technologies, and social customs of a growing nation.

Conclusion: The Seeds of American Cigar Culture

The story of tobacco and cigars in early America is far more than a tale of agriculture and commerce—it is the story of a nation finding its identity. From the tobacco fields of colonial Virginia to the frontier saloons of the American West, cigars and tobacco helped shape the economic, social, and cultural landscape of a growing nation.

The journey began with John Rolfe's experimental tobacco cultivation in Jamestown and reached new heights with Lt. Col. Israel Putnam's introduction of Cuban cigars to New England. Through times of peace and war, cigars became increasingly woven into the fabric of American life. Military conflicts—the War of 1812, the Mexican-American War, and especially the Civil War—spread cigar culture across the nation, while entrepreneurial spirits like Roger G. Sullivan transformed local craftsmanship into thriving enterprises.

The westward expansion brought new dimensions to American cigar culture, blending Spanish colonial traditions with frontier pragmatism. In saloons and trading posts from Kansas to California, cigars became symbols of status and sophistication, even in the roughest frontier towns. The stories of Wild Bill Hickok, Wyatt Earp, and countless other Western figures became inseparable from the cigars they famously enjoyed.

By the dawn of the Industrial Revolution, America had become more than just a tobacco-growing nation. It had transformed into a cigar-making powerhouse, with distinct regional traditions from the artisanal workshops of New England to the immigrant-operated factories of San Francisco. The stage was set for the golden age of American cigar manufacturing, which would transform this craft industry into one of the nation's largest commercial enterprises.

As we move into the next chapter, we will explore how industrialization, immigration, and innovation revolutionized cigar production in the late 19th century, creating an industry that would produce billions of cigars annually and employ hundreds of thousands of Americans. The seeds planted in colonial soil would grow into a truly American industry, one that would help define the nation's character for generations to come.

"What does labor want?
More schoolhouses and less jails;
more books and less arsenals;
more learning and less vice."

— SAMUEL GOMPERS, founding president of
the American Federation of Labor

———

Gompers learned to organize on the floor of a New York cigar factory. The American labor movement was born among cigarmakers decades before the automobile, the assembly line, or the mass strikes of the steel and auto eras would reshape American industrial relations.

CHAPTER 2

The Rise of the American
Cigar Industry

The Industrial Revolution | The period between 1870 and 1920 was a defining era in American history—a period of unprecedented economic expansion, sweeping social change, and technological breakthroughs. Emerging from the devastation of the Civil War, the United States rapidly transformed into the world's leading industrial power. Railroads, steel, and mechanized manufacturing reshaped the economy, while urbanization and large-scale immigration altered the fabric of American society. This era saw the rise of corporate capitalism, labor movements, and consumer culture, laying the foundation for the modern economic landscape.

Technological Innovation and Industrial Expansion

The late 19th century witnessed an explosion of technological advancements that revolutionized industry and daily life. Thomas Edison's electric light bulb (1879) and Alexander Graham Bell's telephone (1876) transformed communication and infrastructure. American steel output rose dramatically over these decades. By 1900, the United States was producing over 10 million tons annually, more than England and Germany combined.

Railroads became the backbone of this transformation. The completion of the Transcontinental Railroad (1869) connected the coasts, yet it was the rapid expansion of over 254,000 miles of track by 1916 that truly unified the national economy. Rail networks linked rural production centers to booming industrial cities, facilitating the movement of goods, labor, and capital at an unprecedented scale.

The Rise of Corporate Power and Mass Production

The late 19th century saw the emergence of large-scale corporate capitalism, as industry titans like John D. Rockefeller (Standard Oil) and J.P. Morgan (finance and industrial consolidation) pioneered new business models. The rise of trusts and monopolies concentrated economic power in a few hands, reshaping industries from oil and steel to railroads and finance. In 1901, Morgan orchestrated the creation of U.S. Steel, marking the birth of the first billion-dollar corporation.

The factory system underwent a profound transformation with the introduction of scientific management, pioneered by Frederick Winslow Taylor, which emphasized efficiency and mechanized workflows. The implementation of assembly line techniques—most famously in Henry Ford's automobile plants (1913)—revolutionized production, making goods more affordable and accessible to the growing middle class.

Immigration, Labor, and the Working Class Struggle

The rapid industrial expansion created an insatiable demand for labor, fueling one of the largest waves of immigration in U.S. history. Between 1870 and 1920, more than 25 million immigrants arrived, primarily from Southern and Eastern Europe, settling in cities like New York, Chicago, and Pittsburgh. These workers provided the backbone of the industrial economy but often faced dangerous conditions, low wages, and long hours.

In response, the labor movement gained momentum. Unions such as the American Federation of Labor (AFL, founded in 1886) and the Industrial Workers of the World (IWW, 1905) fought for better wages, shorter workdays, and improved safety standards. Major labor conflicts—such as the Homestead Strike (1892) and Pullman Strike (1894)—highlighted the growing tensions between industrial capital and labor.

Urbanization and the Birth of Consumer Culture

Industrialization triggered large-scale migration to cities, fundamentally altering American society. In 1870, only 25 percent of Americans lived in urban areas; by 1920, this had nearly doubled to 50 percent. Cities like Chicago grew from 299,000 residents in 1870 to 2.2 million by 1920, creating new social dynamics and economic opportunities.

The rise of mass production and department stores signaled the emergence of a consumer economy. Retail giants like Marshall Field's (Chicago) and Macy's (New York) made previously unattainable goods widely available, shifting American culture toward a lifestyle of purchasing and leisure. The advertising industry boomed, shaping consumer habits and brand loyalty.

The U.S. as an Industrial and Global Power

By 1914, the United States had surpassed Great Britain, Germany, and France combined in industrial output, solidifying its status as the world's foremost economic power. The outbreak of World War I (1914–1918) further accelerated American industrial production, setting the stage for the nation's emergence as a global economic and political leader.

In summary, the Industrial Revolution between 1870 and 1920 was far more than a period of economic expansion. It was a fundamental reshaping of society. Technological progress, mass production, immigration, and urbanization transformed the United States from an agrarian society into an industrial powerhouse. This new era of wealth and consumerism was also one of inequality and labor struggles, with the country balancing progress and conflict as it entered the 20th century.

This transformation set the stage for the rise of the American cigar industry, which mirrored the broader economic and social changes of the time. The next section explores how industrialization, immigration, and consumer demand fueled the golden age of cigar manufacturing in the United States.

The Smoke of a Changing Nation

In the decades following the Civil War, a simple rolled tobacco leaf became far more than a consumer product. The cigar emerged as a complex cultural artifact that would tell the story of America's transformation—a story of immigration, industrialization, economic mobility, and social change.

Between 1870 and 1920, American tobacco consumption dramatically increased, transforming from a luxury reserved for wealthy gentlemen to a widely accessible commodity that crossed racial, class, and ethnic boundaries. By 1900, just three cities—New York, Philadelphia, and Tampa—were producing over 2 billion cigars annually, a figure that represented only part of the nation's total cigar production, illustrating the industry's explosive growth and widespread cultural significance.[3]

The cigar industry represented a microcosm of American industrial development. It was a world where immigrant workers from Cuba, Spain, Italy, and Eastern Europe transformed raw tobacco into cultural symbols. Their hands did more than roll leaves—they wove together economic opportunity, cultural preservation, and the complex narrative of American identity.

Technological innovation, labor struggles, global trade networks, and shifting cultural perceptions converged in the humble cigar. From the tenement workshops of New York to the vast tobacco fields of Connecticut, from the mechanized factories of Pennsylvania to the hand-rolling traditions of Tampa's Ybor City, cigars told a story larger than themselves.

---

[3] Throughout this book, a distinction between machine-made and hand-rolled cigars will be made whenever possible. However, as mechanization became more integrated into cigar production, it grew increasingly difficult to determine which cigars were entirely handmade, partially machine-assisted, or fully machine-produced.

Historical market data on cigar production methods is often scarce and inconsistent. Industry records from earlier periods lacked sophistication, making it challenging to track production techniques with precision. The cigar industry itself was highly diverse—a mosaic of large factory operations, small artisanal workshops, and family-run businesses. While many were concentrated in major metropolitan hubs, others were scattered across the country, including in Western territories.

It was only during the cigar boom of the 1990s that the market became clearly segmented, drawing a firm distinction between machine-made and hand-rolled premium cigars—both in consumer perception and industry analysis. For much of history, however, smokers—particularly working-class consumers—viewed cigars primarily in terms of affordability rather than production method. While price often correlated with how a cigar was made, this distinction was not always captured in market data at the time.

This chapter explores how a simple tobacco product became a lens through which we can understand the dramatic social and economic transformations of turn-of-the-century America. It is a story of human ingenuity, cultural resilience, and the perpetual reinvention that defines the American experience.

The Industrial Boom: How Cigars Became a Mass Market Staple

The transformation of cigar consumption in post-Civil War America represents one of the most remarkable industrial and cultural shifts of the 19th century. What had once been a luxury reserved for the wealthy became a democratic commodity that crossed social boundaries, reflecting the broader economic and demographic changes sweeping the nation.

Surging Demand & Changing Consumer Habits

The decades following the Civil War witnessed an unprecedented economic metamorphosis. Industrialization, urbanization, and rising wages created a new economic landscape where discretionary spending became possible for a growing working and middle class. Cigars emerged as a symbol of this newfound economic mobility—an affordable luxury that signaled both personal achievement and social belonging.

By the late 19th century, cigar production had dramatically expanded. By 1895, the United States had at least 30,000 cigar manufacturing operations—a figure that would grow to roughly 80,000 by 1905 as small family shops proliferated alongside large factories — transforming what was once a luxury into an accessible commodity. For the first time, a worker in a textile mill or a clerk in a burgeoning urban office could afford the same type of cigar once exclusively enjoyed by businessmen and politicians.

The railroad played a crucial role in this widespread availability of tobacco. Vast transportation networks allowed cigar manufacturers to distribute their products far beyond traditional urban markets. Small-town general stores in Kansas, saloons in Montana, and hotels in Louisiana all began stocking a variety of cigars, making these products accessible to previously underserved markets.

The cigar industry's labor force was remarkably substantial for its time. Contemporary historical sources suggest that cigar manufacturing employed approximately 126,000 workers in 1900, representing a significant industrial workforce during an era of rapid economic transformation. While precise documentation requires additional research, available census and labor records indicate the cigar industry was a major employer in the early 20th century—approximately 0.5 percent of the total US workforce of 24 million.

For comparative perspective, today's automotive manufacturing *directly* employs about 308,000 workers, which is only about 0.19 percent of the current US workforce of 161 million. This statistical breakdown reveals that the cigar industry was proportionally more significant in 1900 than automotive manufacturing is today.[4]

The workforce was also notably diverse and progressive for its era. By 1900, women constituted 47 percent of cigar makers—a remarkable level of female participation in manufacturing at the time. Beyond the cigar industry, child labor was widespread, with the 1900 census counting 1.75 million children aged 10–15 as 'gainful workers.' In 1905, approximately 80,000 cigar-manufacturing businesses existed, most of them small family operations that were crucial economic engines for immigrant communities.

The scale of this transformation can be measured in concrete numbers.

BY THE NUMBERS: The American Cigar Industry's Transformation 1870-1920

Industry Growth
• Annual Production: Dramatic increase from approximately
  200 million to several billion cigars (1870-1920) *
• From Small Manufacturers: 15,000+ in 1870 and 80,000 in 1905
  To Large Manufacturers: 8,000 in 1920 with top 20 companies producing 60% of all cigars **

Price Points (1900)
• Budget cigars: 2-5 cents

---

[4] It is important to point out that these two industries, as a whole, should only be very carefully compared. The automotive industry's comprehensive employment structure, including its extensive supply chain and spillover industries, is far more complex and larger in scale than the cigar-making industry ever was. Regardless, this much is clear: the numbers cited above vividly illustrate the significant scale of the cigar industry employment during this historical period.

30

- Popular brands: 5-10 cents
- Premium domestic: 25-50 cents
- Imported Havanas: 50 cents to $1.50

Major Production Centers (Annual Output 1900)
- New York City: 1.2 billion cigars (23,000 workers)
- Philadelphia: 800 million cigars (12,000 workers)
- Tampa: 250 million cigars (10,000 workers)

Worker Demographics (1900)
- Total industry employment: 126,000 workers
- Immigrant workers: 70%
- Average weekly wages for skilled hand-rollers: $12-18

* Note: Historical records show varying production estimates but consistently reflect industry growth. As mechanization expanded in the late 19th and early 20th centuries, reported figures often failed to distinguish between machine-made and handcrafted cigars—a trend that continued into the 1990s, complicating assessments of premium versus mass-produced cigars (see Endnote 2, page 174).
** This transformation illustrates the broader trend of industrial consolidation and mechanization in early 20th-century American manufacturing, with production scaling from 200 million to several billion cigars between 1870 and 1920.

This unprecedented growth laid the foundation for America's first national cigar brands, transforming local manufacturers into household names and fundamentally reshaping how Americans consumed and perceived cigars.

Technological and Economic Innovations

Several technological and economic innovations facilitated this dramatic expansion. Improvements in agricultural techniques increased tobacco yields, while advances in curing and processing methods enhanced the quality and consistency of tobacco products. The development of more efficient transportation—particularly railroads and steamships— dramatically reduced shipping costs and expanded market reach.

Tobacco Landscape: Domestic and Global

The United States emerged as a global tobacco powerhouse during this period. The 1900 Census Bulletin identified New York, Pennsylvania, Ohio, Florida, and Illinois as the leading states in cigar and cigarette production. Connecticut's tobacco industry was particularly notable, with the Connecticut River Valley hosting numerous cigar farms and contributing high-quality wrapper leaves to the national market. These regions developed sophisticated cultivation techniques that produced distinctive tobacco varieties, each offering unique flavor profiles that distinguished American cigars.

Simultaneously, international trade networks brought premium tobaccos from Cuba, Sumatra, and the Philippines. These imported leaves complemented domestic varieties, allowing American cigar makers to create complex, nuanced blends that appealed to increasingly discerning consumers.

Labor and Manufacturing Dynamics

The cigar industry's expansion was fundamentally a human story—driven by waves of immigrant labor that brought sophisticated craftsmanship to American manufacturing. Cities like New York, Philadelphia, and Tampa became crucibles of cigar production, where Cuban, Spanish, Italian, and Eastern European workers transformed small workshops into industrial enterprises.

These factories were microcosms of America's industrial revolution. Some employed fewer than ten workers, operating as family businesses, while others housed hundreds of skilled rollers producing thousands of cigars daily. Despite challenging working conditions—hot, crowded spaces with minimal ventilation—these factories represented opportunities for economic advancement for immigrant communities.

The hand-rolling process remained dominant through the late 19th century, a testament to the skill of workers who, as is still the case in modern cigar production, could likely produce 100 or more cigars per day. As historical records indicate, cigar making was a piece-work job where workers were paid based on their production, highlighting the craft's labor-intensive nature. This method ensured a level of quality and craftsmanship that machine production would later challenge.

Economic and Cultural Significance

More than an industrial product, cigars became a cultural artifact that reflected America's complex social dynamics. They were markers of status, tools of social interaction, and symbols of personal freedom. From working-class laborers to emerging corporate executives, cigar smoking transcended traditional social boundaries.

By the turn of the century, the American cigar industry had transformed from a cottage industry to a sophisticated, nationwide economic force—a change that mirrored the nation's own rapid development.

While the industrial boom created unprecedented demand for cigars, it also fundamentally transformed how these products were made, traded, and consumed on a global scale. Understanding this transformation requires a deeper look at the complex ecosystem that emerged around cigar production and distribution.

The State of the Industry

The American cigar industry of the late 19th and early 20th centuries was not an isolated phenomenon, but a complex global network of trade, innovation, and cultural exchange. At its heart was a delicate dance between domestic production and international influences, technological disruption and traditional craftsmanship.

The Global Tobacco Landscape

Cuba stood at the epicenter of this intricate world. More than a mere tobacco producer, the island was a mythical source of the world's finest leaves, a reputation that transformed tobacco from a simple agricultural product into a geopolitical commodity. American cigar manufacturers viewed Cuban tobacco with a combination of reverence and strategic calculation.

The Spanish colonial system had long controlled tobacco trade, creating intricate networks that connected plantations in Cuba with markets in Europe and, increasingly, the United States. These networks didn't just move tobacco; they moved culture, techniques, and economic possibilities.

By the 1890s, American tobacco interests had begun to reshape these traditional pathways. The McKinley Tariff of 1890 was a calculated economic maneuver that would fundamentally alter international tobacco dynamics. By raising import duties, the United States simultaneously protected domestic growers and signaled its emerging economic power.

Technological Transformation

Technological innovation became the true revolution of the cigar industry. Agricultural techniques transformed tobacco cultivation from an art passed through generations to a scientifically optimized process. Crop rotation, soil analysis, and selective breeding allowed farmers to produce higher-quality leaves with unprecedented consistency.

In Connecticut's river valleys and Pennsylvania's rolling farmlands, agricultural scientists worked alongside traditional farmers. They developed strain varieties that could withstand different climates, resist disease, and produce more robust flavors. These were not mere agricultural improvements, but a fundamental reimagining of tobacco as a precision crop.

Processing technologies evolved equally dramatically. Curing barns, once dependent on traditional wood-fired methods, incorporated temperature-controlled environments. Humidity and air circulation became as important as the type of wood used in curing. These innovations allowed for more consistent flavor profiles and reduced the risk of crop failure.

The Economic Ecosystem

The economic structure of the cigar industry was a marvel of complexity. Small family-run operations existed alongside massive industrial producers, creating an ecosystem that was simultaneously traditional and modern. A cigar factory in Tampa might employ hundreds of workers using techniques brought from Cuba, while a mechanized operation in New York could produce thousands of cigars hourly.

Labor represented a critical economic variable. Immigrant workers were not just laborers but skilled artisans who brought generational knowledge. Their economic value extended far beyond simple wage labor; they were repositories of complex cultural and technical knowledge.

Trade networks became increasingly sophisticated. Railroads and steamships transformed distribution, allowing cigars produced in small urban workshops to reach rural markets thousands of miles away. What had once been a local product became a national commodity.

Economic Impact

By 1900, the cigar industry represented more than a manufacturing sector—it was a significant economic driver. The industry employed tens of thousands, generated substantial tax revenues, and played a crucial role in urban economic development, particularly in immigrant communities. The economic ripple effects were profound. Cigar production stimulated related industries—from packaging to transportation, from agricultural equipment to advertising. A single cigar represented a complex economic artifact, embodying labor, innovation, and global trade.

The industry's economic significance went beyond numbers. Cigars represented economic mobility, a tangible symbol of the American dream. For immigrant communities, cigar manufacturing was a pathway to economic integration and social advancement.

A Transformative Era

The early decades of the 20th century represented a pivotal moment. Traditional craft met industrial efficiency, global networks intersected with local production, and technological innovation reshaped an ancient agricultural practice.

The American cigar was more than a product. It was a testament to a nation in transformation—complex, dynamic, and perpetually reinventing itself.

Cigar Cities: America's Manufacturing Hubs

The rise of the American cigar industry was not a monolithic narrative, but a tapestry of regional innovations, immigrant entrepreneurship, and cultural exchange. Each manufacturing hub represented a unique ecosystem of tobacco production, reflecting the complex social and economic dynamics of late 19th-century America.

New York & Pennsylvania: The Crucibles of Cigar Manufacturing

By the late 1800s, the northeastern United States had emerged as the epicenter of cigar production, with New York City and Philadelphia standing as titans of the industry. By 1900, the production landscape was clearly defined: New York City led the nation, producing 1.2 billion cigars annually with 23,000 workers, far outpacing Philadelphia's 800 million cigars and 12,000 workers.

These were not merely industrial sites, but intricate social networks where immigrant communities found economic opportunity and cultural preservation. Family-run shops dominated the landscape, with many operating out of tenement workshops and small storefronts. These businesses were more than economic enterprises; they were lifelines for newly arrived immigrants seeking economic mobility.

The immigrant composition of these factories told a rich story of American diversity. German, Eastern European, and Jewish immigrants brought not just labor, but sophisticated craftsmanship and cultural traditions. In the crowded tenement workshops of New York's Lower East Side and the industrial corridors of Pennsylvania's Lancaster and York, these communities transformed cigar manufacturing into an art form.

The Economic Ecosystem of Immigrant Labor

Each immigrant group brought distinct skills and cultural practices to cigar production. German immigrants, with their precision engineering backgrounds, often managed factory operations. Eastern European Jews, many with trading and merchant backgrounds, developed distribution networks and marketing strategies. The result was a dynamic, innovative industry that was far more than a simple labor market.

Tampa: The Emergence of "Cigar City"

If New York and Pennsylvania represented the industrial north, Tampa embodied the multicultural spirit of cigar manufacturing in the American south. The story of Tampa's transformation is fundamentally the story of Vicente Martinez-Ybor, a Cuban tobacco baron whose vision would reshape an entire city.

In the 1880s, Martinez-Ybor made a pivotal decision to relocate his cigar operations from Key West to Tampa. This was not merely a business move, but a complex negotiation of economic opportunity, political landscape, and cultural preservation. Ybor City emerged as a testament to the transnational nature of the cigar industry.

Tampa's geographical advantage was critical. Its proximity to Cuba ensured a steady, high-quality tobacco supply. But more importantly, the city attracted a diverse workforce of Cuban, Spanish, and Afro-Cuban workers who brought generations of cigar-making expertise. By 1929, Tampa hosted over 200 cigar factories, earning its legendary nickname, "Cigar City."

The Cultural Significance of Ybor City

Ybor City[5] was more than an industrial district; it was a living, breathing community. Social clubs, mutual aid societies, and cultural institutions flourished alongside the factories. Workers were not just laborers but active participants in a vibrant, transnational community that maintained strong connections to their ancestral homelands.

This thriving community was not just shaping the cigar industry—it exemplified a broader shift in production. As factories across the country increased output, a seismic change was underway: cigars, once a luxury of the elite, were becoming an affordable pleasure for the masses.

The 5-Cent Revolution: Democratizing Luxury

The emergence of the 5-cent cigar represented a profound democratization of a once-exclusive luxury. Mechanization, efficient labor practices, and economies of scale transformed cigars from elite commodities to everyday pleasures.

Brands like Cremo, Garcia y Vega, and King Edward became more than commercial products—they were symbols of a changing American social landscape. A worker in a Chicago factory, a clerk in a New York office, or a farmer in rural Missouri could now enjoy the same smoking experience previously reserved for the wealthy.

---

[5] Ybor City's designation as the "Cigar Capital of the World" reflects the economic and cultural transformation of American manufacturing in the late 19th century, highlighting the industry's dramatic growth and the role of immigrant entrepreneurship.

These budget cigars were consumed in quintessentially American spaces—saloons that served as community centers, barbershops where local gossip and politics intertwined, and workplaces where a quick smoke represented a moment of personal respite.

The 5-cent cigar was not just a product but a social leveler, a small daily luxury that spoke to the promise of economic mobility and shared experience in an increasingly complex American society.

Cigar workers at the Corral Wodiska factory, Tampa, 1929. Photograph by Burgert Brothers. Tampa-Hillsborough County Public Library System. A lector can be seen on a raised platform, reading to the workers in the upper right-hand corner.

This democratization of luxury was led by ambitious manufacturers who understood that building national brands required more than just affordable prices—it demanded consistent quality, innovative marketing, and efficient distribution. Their success stories would define the industry for generations to come.

The Rise of American Cigar Brands: Creating Icons of the Industry

The late 19th and early 20th centuries saw the emergence of cigar brands that would become household names across America. These weren't just products—they were cultural touchstones that reflected the democratization of luxury and the rise of modern marketing.

Cremo, launched in 1896, quickly became a prominent player in the cigar industry. Manufactured by the American Cigar Company[6], the brand was known for its five-cent cigars and innovative marketing. By the early 1900s, Cremo had become one of America's most successful cigar brands, attaining the largest sales of any cigar in its class. In 1929, the company gained additional attention through a bold advertising campaign that targeted public health concerns, running anti-spitting advertisements in over 100 newspapers. Within two years of its provocative marketing campaign, Cremo had solidified its position as a top-selling cigar brand, demonstrating the power of innovative advertising.

The American Tobacco Company's transformation of White Owl into a national brand demonstrated the power of mass marketing. Originally a small Manhattan brand, White Owl became synonymous with consistent quality at an accessible price point. Their 1920s slogan "Always Good" resonated with consumers seeking reliability in their smoking experience. King Edward cigars, introduced by John H. Swisher & Son in 1918, became the world's most popular cigar brand by the 1940s, largely due to their perfect storm of quality, price, and distribution. Operating from Jacksonville, Florida, Swisher's innovative manufacturing processes allowed them to produce cigars at unprecedented scale while maintaining consistent quality.

Garcia y Vega, established in 1882, represented a crucial bridge between artisanal Cuban traditions and American mass production. Their success proved that heritage and industrial efficiency could coexist, as they maintained elements of traditional craftsmanship while embracing modern manufacturing methods.

Dutch Masters, launched in 1911, cleverly used fine art in their marketing, featuring Rembrandt's famous "Syndics of the Drapers' Guild" on their

---

[6] Note: The American Cigar Company discontinued operations in the early 1950s, nearly 40 years after its parent tobacco conglomerate was dissolved by the U.S. Supreme Court in 1911 due to antitrust violations.

packaging. This sophisticated branding helped position machine-made cigars as culturally refined products, despite their affordable price point.

These brands didn't just sell cigars—they sold American aspirations. Through innovative advertising, consistent quality, and strategic pricing, they transformed cigars from occasional luxuries into daily pleasures for millions of Americans. Their success stories exemplified the broader transformation of the American cigar industry from a craft-based trade into a modern consumer goods sector.

The Fight Against Mechanization: The Human Cost of Industrial Progress

The story of the American cigar industry is fundamentally a human narrative—a complex drama of technological innovation, labor struggle, and economic transformation. As factories sought efficiency, skilled workers fought to preserve not just their livelihoods, but a centuries-old craft that was deeply intertwined with cultural identity and professional pride.

The Technological Disruption

The introduction of cigar-rolling machines represented more than a mere industrial innovation; it was a fundamental shift that would redefine labor, skill, and economic value. In the 1880s, when the first mechanical rollers appeared, they promised unprecedented production efficiency. A skilled hand roller could produce 100-150 cigars per day, while these machines could manufacture hundreds of cigars per hour.

This technological leap was not merely about numbers. It represented a fundamental reimagining of craftsmanship—transforming a nuanced, artistic process into a standardized, mechanical operation. For immigrant workers who had brought generations of rolling expertise from Cuba, Spain, and other tobacco-producing regions, this represented an existential threat.

The Cigar Makers' International Union: A Bastion of Resistance

The Cigar Makers' International Union (CMIU), founded in 1864, emerged as a critical counterforce to industrial mechanization. The union was more than a traditional labor organization—it was a sophisticated social and political movement that understood the broader implications of technological displacement.

The CMIU's strategy was multifaceted. They didn't simply resist machines; they advocated for worker retraining, negotiated protective clauses in employment contracts, and used legal and political channels to slow mechanization. Their leadership understood that preservation of craft required more than street protests—it demanded strategic, long-term thinking.

Though the CMIU's immediate battles seemed localized, they were laying groundwork for a broader reckoning. The union's resistance would echo through generations, culminating in moments of profound social transformation. To fully grasp the magnitude of what was brewing for decade after decade starting in the late 1800s, we can briefly fast forward to about 50 years later....

Racial Dynamics and Labor Struggle

The Charleston Cigar Strike of 1945-46 revealed the complex racial dimensions of labor struggles in the tobacco industry. Led by Black cigar workers in South Carolina, the strike was a powerful testament to the intersectionality of labor rights and racial justice.

These workers confronted not just economic inequality, but a deeply entrenched system of racial segregation. Their demands for higher wages and union recognition were revolutionary acts in a Jim Crow society. Though the strike resulted in modest wage increases, it illuminated the systemic racial and economic injustices that had been shaping the industry since the early 1900s.

The Machines Advance: An Unstoppable Industrial Tide

Despite heroic resistance, mechanization proved inevitable. By the time of World War I, mechanical rollers had become widespread. The economics were brutally simple: machines could produce cigars at a fraction of the human labor cost, and consumer demand for affordable cigars continued to grow.

By the 1920s, a clear transformation had occurred. Lower-cost cigars were now predominantly machine-made, while hand-rolled cigars became luxury items. Small workshops, once the backbone of cigar production, became obsolete.

This was not merely an industrial shift but a profound cultural transformation. Immigrant communities that had built their economic and social identities around cigar rolling were forced to adapt. Skills passed down through generations suddenly lost their economic value.

The mechanization of cigar production symbolized broader changes in American industrial society—the ongoing tension between human skill and technological efficiency, between artisanal tradition and mass production.

A Legacy of Resilience

The story of labor in the cigar industry is ultimately a story of human resilience. Workers didn't simply disappear; they adapted, found new opportunities, and continued to shape American industrial culture. The unions they built, the struggles they waged, and the communities they maintained would influence labor movements for generations to come.

As labor battles raged in factories and workshops, the products themselves told their own story of social transformation. The cigars Americans chose to smoke reflected not just personal taste, but the broader economic and cultural changes reshaping society.

WHAT DID THEY SMOKE?

A Connoisseur's Journey Through Early 20th Century Cigar Culture

The humble cigar was far more than a mere tobacco product in early 20th century America—it was a passport to social identity, a marker of economic status, and a silent storyteller of personal ambition. From the bustling streets of New York to the humid factories of Tampa, cigars wove themselves into the very fabric of American life.

The smoking landscape was sharply divided between premium and popular offerings. For those with means, hand-rolled premium cigars like the Havana Especiales and La Palina represented the pinnacle of refinement. These weren't just smokes but carefully curated statements of success, selected to impress in boardrooms and gentlemen's clubs. A hand-rolled Cuban-wrapper cigar spoke volumes about its owner's taste and standing, making each puff a declaration of achievement.

The art of selection went beyond brand names. Connoisseurs developed sophisticated palates for regional tobacco varieties. The delicate, light leaves of Connecticut Valley tobacco offered subtle, refined flavors, while the robust, dark Pennsylvania Broadleaf provided rich, bold profiles. Understanding these distinctions became a mark of sophistication—the ability to discuss a cigar's terroir marked one as truly cultured.

The ritual of smoking itself evolved into a carefully choreographed social performance. In private clubs, hotel lounges, and after-dinner gatherings, the selection, cutting, and lighting of a cigar became a display of cultural literacy. Railroad smoking cars and hotel lounges became stages where men performed their status through their choice of cigars and their knowledge of proper smoking etiquette.

Yet cigars weren't confined to elite spaces. In barbershops and neighborhood saloons, working men gathered to enjoy their smokes, creating their own rituals and traditions. Here, cigars served as social lubricants, facilitating conversations and connections across class lines. A shared smoke could bridge social divisions, creating moments of camaraderie in an otherwise stratified society.

The smoking ritual carried deeper cultural significance in immigrant communities. For Cuban and Spanish workers in Tampa's Ybor City, or Jewish and Italian craftsmen in New York's workshops, cigars connected them to ancestral traditions of craftsmanship and artisan work while participating in American consumer culture. Each puff maintained a link to their heritage even as they built new lives in America.

This complex social geography of smoking reflected broader tensions in American society. The choice between hand-rolled and machine-made cigars wasn't just about price—it reflected fundamental questions about tradition versus progress, craft versus efficiency, and old world versus new. Every cigar told a story about its smoker's place in this changing landscape.

In the end, the cigar a man chose said something. It was a small, fragrant testament to the American dream—a carefully chosen symbol of who you were, who you wanted to be, and how you wanted others to see you. Whether enjoyed in a mahogany-paneled club or a humble neighborhood bar, each cigar represented a moment of pleasure and possibility in a rapidly transforming nation.

Cultural Representations: Cigars in the American Imagination

The cigar transcended its physical form to become one of America's most potent cultural symbols. In the late 19th and early 20th centuries, it evolved into a sophisticated language of social communication, expressing complex ideas about power, success, and identity in American life.

Literature embraced the cigar as a powerful narrative device. Mark Twain, himself inseparable from his cigars, used them masterfully in his works to reveal character and social standing. In Theodore Dreiser's "The Financier," the protagonist's journey from modest clerk to wealthy businessman is marked by his evolving taste in cigars. Writers understood that a character lighting a fine cigar could wordlessly convey everything from achieved ambition to moral corruption.

The visual arts captured cigars with equally rich symbolism. John Singer Sargent's portraits of Gilded Age industrialists often featured carefully positioned cigars, transforming them into scepters of American power. Political cartoonists wielded the cigar as shorthand for capitalism itself— Thomas Nast's famous depictions of Boss Tweed invariably showed him with an oversized cigar, suggesting both luxury and corruption.

Early advertising pioneers recognized the cigar's unique cultural power. The Dutch Masters campaign revolutionized tobacco marketing by appropriating classical art, suggesting that smoking their cigars connected consumers to European cultural sophistication. White Owl's "Always Good" campaigns of the 1920s presented the cigar as a marker of dependable American masculinity, while La Palina's advertisements featured sophisticated urban settings that promised social elevation through consumption.

Popular entertainment seized upon the cigar's dramatic potential. In vaudeville[7], the difference between a character chomping on a cheap stogie or delicately puffing a fine Havana instantly established their social position. Early cinema magnified these associations—from Charlie Chaplin's ironic use of cigars to mock the wealthy, to the gangster films of the 1930s where cigars became menacing symbols of illicit power.

In the smoky underworld of Prohibition-era Chicago, cigars became more than mere tobacco—they were potent symbols of power, wealth, and criminal sophistication. Al Capone, the infamous gangster whose name would become synonymous with organized crime, exemplified this cultural iconography. Known as "Scarface," Capone was rarely seen without an expensive cigar, which served as a visual proclamation of his illicit empire. His flamboyant style, marked by tailored suits and ostentatious jewelry, was complemented by the ever-present cigar—a prop that signaled both his economic dominance and his brazen defiance of social norms. So embedded was Capone's association with cigars that an entire brand of cigarillos would later bear his name, immortalizing the connection between tobacco and criminal luxury.

While Capone's cigars represented a performative display of criminal power, for many immigrant communities, these rolled leaves told a far more nuanced story of cultural survival and collective identity.

---

[7] Vaudeville was a popular form of variety entertainment in the United States from the late 19th century to the early 20th century. It featured a mix of acts, such as comedians, musicians, dancers, magicians, and other performers, often in a series of short, diverse segments. Vaudeville shows were staged in theaters and were a major form of entertainment before the rise of film and television.

For immigrant communities, cigars carried additional layers of meaning. In the cigar-making districts of Tampa and New York, the skilled craft of rolling represented not just employment but cultural preservation. The lectores (readers) in cigar factories, reading newspapers and literature to workers in Spanish while they rolled, transformed factory floors into spaces of cultural resistance and education.

The political symbolism of cigars proved especially potent. Editorial cartoonists used cigars to represent everything from imperial ambition (in Spanish-American War imagery) to corporate monopoly (in anti-trust illustrations). The "smoke-filled room"—a term coined after the 1920 Republican convention (as we shall see)—became shorthand for political dealmaking, with cigars representing both power and its concealment.

Yet the cigar's meaning continued to evolve, shifting with America's social transformations. When cigarettes began dominating popular culture, cigars increasingly symbolized either old-world tradition or counter-cultural rebellion. The image of the cigar-smoker shifted from a symbol of aspiration to a target of criticism, reflecting changing attitudes toward wealth and power.

By the 1920s, the cigar had become one of America's most layered cultural texts—an object that could simultaneously represent immigrant craft traditions, industrial might, political power, and social mobility. In literature, art, advertising, and popular culture, it functioned as a remarkably flexible symbol of American ambitions and anxieties, making visible the nation's complex relationships with wealth, power, and identity.

Women and Cigars: Challenging Social Boundaries

The story of labor and mechanization wasn't just about male workers fighting to preserve their craft. Women, too, played a crucial role in this industrial drama, challenging not only economic structures but deeply entrenched social boundaries.

The world of cigars in late 19th and early 20th century America was predominantly masculine—or so the standard narrative suggests. Yet the

Mark Twain Portrait (Late 19th century). Few cultural icons embodied the American love affair with cigars as completely as Samuel Clemens, better known as Mark Twain. This photograph captures Twain in his quintessential pose—a cigar held with the casual confidence of a man who once famously declared, "If I cannot smoke in heaven, then I shall not go." More than a mere accessory, the cigar was central to Twain's public persona, symbolizing wit, rebellion, and a distinctly American brand of irreverence. He was known to smoke up to 300 cigars a month, transforming the act of smoking from a personal habit into a form of literary and personal performance that helped define the cultural mystique of the cigar in late 19th-century America.

real story was far more complex, revealing how women navigated, challenged, and transformed the cigar industry in ways that defied simple categorization.

In the cigar factories of New York, Philadelphia, and Tampa, women were not peripheral figures but critical participants in the industry's economic ecosystem. Immigrant women—Jewish, Italian, Cuban—worked alongside men in rolling rooms, their skilled hands producing the very products that would become cultural icons. These were not just laborers, but skilled artisans who brought generational knowledge and precision to their craft.

The labor dynamics were intricate. While women were often paid less than their male counterparts, they were integral to the industry's success. In many immigrant communities, women's wages were crucial to family economic survival. Their work in cigar factories represented more than economic necessity—it was a form of social mobility and cultural adaptation.

Social perceptions of women and tobacco were deeply contradictory. Public discourse simultaneously glamorized and criticized women's relationship with smoking, casting it as an act of defiance against traditional femininity. A woman smoking a cigar was not merely indulging in a luxury—it was a bold rejection of societal norms, a declaration of personal autonomy that blurred the boundaries between power, pleasure, and rebellion.

Advertising and popular culture reflected these complex dynamics. Early tobacco marketing rarely depicted women directly, but when they did, the images were rich with complex symbolic meaning. Women were alternately portrayed as temptresses, modern rebels, or moral dangers—never simply as consumers or workers.

The racial and class dimensions added further complexity. Working-class women and women of color had different relationships with tobacco compared to their middle and upper-class counterparts. For many, tobacco work represented economic opportunity, while for others, tobacco consumption was a form of social rebellion.

By the early 20th century, women were increasingly visible in tobacco consumption. The emergence of cigarettes—seen as more "feminine" than cigars—provided a new avenue for challenging social expectations. But cigar-smoking women continued to exist, defying simple categorizations of gender and social behavior.

These women were not passive subjects of historical change, but active agents who reshaped industrial and social landscapes. Their stories reveal how gender boundaries were constantly negotiated, challenged, and reimagined in the crucible of industrial America.

The cigar was never just a product. For women, it was a multifaceted symbol of economic survival, social commentary, and personal expression—a small but powerful means of challenging the very structures that sought to constrain them.

Conclusion: The Cigar as a Mirror of American Transformation

By the 1920s, the cigar had become more than a product—it was a living chronicle of American metamorphosis. What began as a luxury item had transformed into a democratic commodity, a small, rolled artifact that captured the complex rhythms of a nation in perpetual motion.

The story of the American cigar was fundamentally a story of human movement and adaptation. Immigrant hands that rolled tobacco leaves were writing a new national narrative, one puff at a time. They were not just manufacturing a product, but constructing possibilities—economic, cultural, and personal.

Technological innovation, labor struggles, and global trade networks had reshaped an entire industry. The cigar stood at the intersection of these profound changes—a symbol of both tradition and radical reinvention. From the hand-rolling traditions of Ybor City to the mechanized factories of the Northeast, cigars reflected America's restless spirit of transformation.

Yet the most profound changes were yet to come. As this chapter closes, the cigar prepares to enter a new arena—the halls of political power. The "smoke-filled rooms" of the next chapter shall reveal how this humble tobacco product would become a language of political negotiation, a tool of diplomacy, and a symbol of leadership.

"Harding of Ohio was chosen by a group of men in
a smoke-filled room early today."

— KIRKE L. SIMPSON, Associated Press dispatch from the
Republican National Convention, Chicago, June 12, 1920

———

Simpson's wire-service line entered the American political vocabulary almost
overnight. The phrase "smoke-filled room" became permanent shorthand for
the way real power moved in American politics—not in the chambers where
laws were debated, but in the suites where cigars were lit and the decisions had
already been made.

CHAPTER 3

Smoke-Filled Rooms &
The Politics of Power

The Gilded Age and Progressive Era (1870-1920) | The period between 1870 and 1920 was an era of paradox—unprecedented economic expansion and political transformation coexisted with stark inequality, systemic corruption, and intense social struggle. Industrial capitalism created vast fortunes for a handful of elite figures, while millions of workers endured grueling conditions in factories, mines, and railroads. Cities swelled with immigrants seeking opportunity, yet they often found themselves facing economic and social hardships. Meanwhile, the corridors of power—whether in corporate boardrooms or political backrooms—became the arenas where monumental decisions were made behind closed doors, in the haze of cigar smoke and whispered negotiations.

The Concentration of Wealth and Corporate Power

By 1890, the top 1 percent of Americans controlled nearly 40 percent of the nation's wealth, marking one of the most extreme economic divides in U.S. history. Industrial magnates such as John D. Rockefeller (Standard Oil), Andrew Carnegie (steel), and J.P. Morgan (finance and railroads) built vast monopolies, reshaping the economy with little government oversight. Rockefeller's Standard Oil controlled over 90 percent of U.S. oil production by 1904, and Carnegie's steel empire symbolized industrial consolidation at its peak.

The doctrine of laissez-faire capitalism and weak antitrust enforcement allowed the rise of trusts and monopolies, granting corporations more power than many government institutions. Company towns—where workers relied entirely on their employers for housing, wages, and even access to basic necessities—became common, reinforcing corporate dominance over everyday life.

The Labor Struggle: Industry vs. the Working Class

The rise of industrial capitalism came at an immense human cost. Workweeks often exceeded 60 hours, wages remained low, and hazardous working conditions were commonplace. The Triangle Shirtwaist Factory fire (1911), which killed 146 workers—mostly immigrant women—due to locked factory doors, became a symbol of unchecked industrial exploitation.

Labor unions emerged as a formidable counterforce to corporate dominance. Organizations like the Knights of Labor (1869) and the American Federation of Labor (1886) fought for shorter workdays, child labor restrictions, and workplace safety. Major strikes—such as the Homestead Strike (1892) and Pullman Strike (1894)—led to violent clashes, often with federal troops intervening on behalf of corporations.

Political Machines and the Corruption of Power

The "smoke-filled rooms" of political machines became the hidden battlegrounds of American democracy, where backroom deals and party loyalty often determined who held power. Tammany Hall, New York's infamous political machine, provided jobs, legal aid, and social services to immigrants in exchange for unwavering political support.

One of the most notorious figures, William "Boss" Tweed, controlled New York's political apparatus in the 1860s and 1870s, embezzling an estimated $200 million (nearly $4 billion today) through elaborate kickback schemes. These urban machines blended corruption with social services, ensuring the loyalty of the working class while reinforcing undemocratic practices.

The Great War and the Cigar Industry: Labor, Demand, and Change

World War I (1914–1918) reshaped America's labor force, including the cigar industry. With thousands of young men drafted, factories faced labor shortages. Women took on expanded roles in cigar rolling, marking an early shift in workforce demographics. Older workers and immigrants also became essential to keeping production lines running.

At the same time, wartime demand for tobacco surged. The U.S. military provided cigars and cigarettes to soldiers, reinforcing tobacco's place in American culture. However, cigarettes, easier to distribute and smoke in trenches, began to eclipse cigars in popularity—a shift with lasting consequences.

Mechanization accelerated as factories sought to compensate for labor shortages, a trend that continued postwar. Returning soldiers needed jobs, but the cigar industry, increasingly reliant on machines, could not absorb them all. Meanwhile, the rise of cigarette production reshaped consumer preferences, signaling the beginning of the cigar industry's gradual decline from its golden age dominance.

The Progressive Movement: A Challenge to the Old Order

As corporate power and political corruption grew, the Progressive movement pushed for social and political reform. Figures such as Theodore Roosevelt, Woodrow Wilson, and activists like Jane Addams championed policies to curb corporate excess, expand democracy, and improve working conditions. Key reforms included:

- Antitrust legislation – The Sherman Antitrust Act (1890) sought to break up monopolies.
- Labor protections – Child labor laws and workplace safety regulations took shape.
- Women's suffrage – The 19th Amendment (1920) granted women the right to vote.
- Direct election of senators – The 17th Amendment (1913) reduced corruption in Senate appointments.
- Prohibition (18th Amendment, 1919) – Aimed at curbing alcohol-related social harms.

Though these reforms reshaped American society, the fight for economic and political justice remained ongoing.

Race, Gender, and the Limits of Progress

Despite economic growth and political reform, racial inequality remained deeply entrenched. Jim Crow laws in the South enforced segregation, and the rise of white supremacist groups sought to maintain racial hierarchies. However, the Great Migration saw hundreds of thousands of African Americans moving north in search of better economic opportunities and basic civil rights.

Gender roles evolved as women increasingly entered the workforce in teaching, nursing, and clerical jobs. By 1920, women made up nearly 25 percent of the workforce, laying the foundation for greater social and political activism.

The Rise of Mass Media and Cultural Shifts

The explosion of mass communication and entertainment further transformed American society.
- Introduced in 1876, the telephone revolutionized communication, and by 1920 nearly 12 million telephones connected people across the country.
- The automobile industry (led by Henry Ford) introduced affordable cars, reshaping urban and rural life.
- Newspapers, magazines, and early film industries created a national culture, influencing politics and social movements.

The period from 1870 to 1920 was one of contradictions. It was an era of rapid industrialization, economic growth, and technological progress—yet also one of corruption, worker exploitation, and deep social inequalities. The struggles between corporate power, labor, political machines, and reformers defined this period, setting the stage for modern American politics and economic policies.

Behind the closed doors of cigar smoke-filled rooms, the deals that shaped America's future were struck—by business leaders, political bosses, and reformers alike. The next section explores how cigars became symbols of power, influence, and prestige in the political and business elite of the Gilded Age and Progressive Era.

The Cigar as a Symbol of Influence: Power's Subtle Ritual

Power in America has never been a mere exercise of formal authority. It has always been a performance, a complex choreography of symbols, gestures, and unspoken languages. And for much of the nation's history, the cigar was its most eloquent translator.

More than a tobacco product, the cigar was a cultural technology—a tool that transformed private conversations into public destinies. In the wood-paneled rooms of Wall Street, the hushed corridors of political conventions, and the intimate spaces of diplomatic negotiations, cigars were never just objects of consumption. They were instruments of influence, silent witnesses to the most consequential moments in American political life.

The Language of Power

In the complex choreography of American power, cigars developed their own sophisticated vocabulary. The brand one chose, the way it was held, when it was lit—each detail carried meaning. A cheap cigar chomped aggressively sent a different message than a premium Cuban savored slowly. These were not mere personal preferences but calculated performances in the theater of influence.

Even the act of offering a cigar was deeply symbolic. It was more than an act of hospitality—it was an invitation into an exclusive network, a gesture of camaraderie, or even a subtle test of allegiance. In the corridors of Congress, a well-placed cigar could signal political alignment just as effectively as a carefully worded speech.

As American society evolved, so did the meanings attached to cigars. In the rough-and-tumble politics of the 19th century, a cigar often signaled working-class populism—a symbol of the urban political machine. By the Gilded Age, it had transformed into a marker of elite sophistication, a status symbol enjoyed by industrial titans and financiers. During the world wars, cigars came to represent stability and resilience in uncertain times.

The Spaces of Influence

Power required its own geography, and cigars helped define it. Exclusive clubs, hotel suites, private dining rooms—these were not just gathering places but stages where influence was quietly exercised. The thick haze of cigar smoke created an atmosphere of exclusivity and camaraderie, transforming ordinary rooms into theaters of power.

These spaces developed their own hierarchies. A seat at the cigar-friendly Palmer House in Chicago carried different weight than membership in New York's Union League Club. Each venue represented a different node in the network of influence, connected by the common thread of tobacco smoke.

The "smoke-filled room" was more than a metaphor. It was a sophisticated political ecosystem where national narratives were constructed, not through public speeches but through carefully calibrated conversations punctuated by the slow burn of premium tobacco.

From the hands of presidents to the boardrooms of industrial titans, cigars carried complex symbolic weight. They represented masculinity, authority, exclusivity—a visual language of power that transcended mere personal habit. A cigar was a statement, a performance, a subtle declaration of social and political status.

These pages explore how a single object serves as a lens through which we understand the intricate mechanisms of American leadership: a story of how smoke, ephemeral and seemingly insubstantial, helped shape the solid architectures of political and economic power.

In the ritual of the cigar, we find a profound truth about American culture: influence is never just about what is said, but about how it is said, where it is said, and the subtle performances that surround those moments of communication.

The Gilded Age: Smoke, Power, and the Architecture of Influence

The cigar was never merely a tobacco product in the Gilded Age. It was a powerful social instrument, a ritual object that facilitated some of the most consequential conversations in American history. In the hushed, wood-paneled rooms of exclusive clubs, beneath chandeliers and behind closed doors, the nation's destiny was being negotiated—one carefully lit cigar at a time.

Private clubs in the late 19th and early 20th centuries were more than gathering spaces; they were the hidden engines of American decision-making. These institutions blurred the lines between business, politics, and social hierarchy, ensuring that the powerful remained interconnected. Membership was an unspoken entry into the corridors of influence, where alliances were forged, deals were struck, and industries were shaped.

Places like New York's Union League Club or Chicago's Palmer House were not simply settings for leisure. They were strategic hubs where a handshake could seal a railroad merger, a casual conversation could set banking policy, and a cigar shared over drinks could realign entire industries. The walls of these clubs absorbed more history than most congressional chambers, bearing silent witness to the rise of American capitalism.

J.P. Morgan embodied this culture of cigar-fueled power. Operating outside formal government channels, he shaped national policy more directly than most cabinet secretaries of his era. His legendary 1907 Wall Street bailout—which stabilized the American financial system in the absence of a central bank—was orchestrated in a setting far removed from public scrutiny. It was not a formal government intervention, but a private summit of banking elites in a smoke-filled room, where Morgan, cigar in hand, dictated the course of the economy.

Industrial titans like Andrew Carnegie and John D. Rockefeller understood this language intimately. Despite their vastly different philosophies on wealth and labor, they shared a common dialect of power—negotiated through the subtle rituals of cigar selection, lighting, and exchange. Carnegie, the advocate of the "Gospel of Wealth," and Rockefeller, the calculating oil baron, both operated within this coded world where cigars were more than luxuries—they were instruments of authority.

Beyond individual magnates, entire industries revolved around cigar culture. The boardroom, increasingly modeled after the private club, became an extension of these spaces of power. A businessman's status was no longer measured solely by his wealth but by the quality of his cigars. The offering of a premium cigar at the negotiation table was not just an act of hospitality—it was a calculated signal of status and intent, a silent but effective form of persuasion.

The Bohemian Club in California, the Metropolitan Club in Washington, D.C., and similar elite institutions became more than social retreats. They were geopolitical laboratories where national strategies were conceived, corporate empires were designed, and the architecture of American industry was sketched out between puffs of expensive Havana tobacco. These were intricate performance spaces where power was negotiated, masculinity was projected, and the unwritten rules of American capitalism were continuously rewritten. The cigar was the prop, the lubricant, and the silent witness to this perpetual drama of ambition and influence.

In the "smoke-filled rooms" of the Gilded Age, history was not just recorded—it was shaped, one carefully timed draw of a cigar at a time.

The "Smoke-Filled Room": Democracy's Hidden Theater

In the sweltering summer of 1920, American democracy revealed its most intimate mechanics—not on a public stage, but in a private suite at Chicago's Blackstone Hotel. The room would become legendary, not for what was seen, but for what was obscured by layers of tobacco smoke and political calculation.

The Republican National Convention was more than a political gathering. It was a complex ritual of power, where the nation's future was decided through whispered conversations and quiet assurances. Warren G. Harding's nomination was not a reflection of public momentum, but a triumph of backroom maneuvering.

When Associated Press reporter Kirke Simpson described the scene—"Harding of Ohio was chosen by a group of men in a smoke-filled room early today"—he captured more than a single event. The phrase "smoke-filled room" entered the American political lexicon, becoming shorthand for the secretive, elite-driven processes that often shaped governance. More than a literal description, it symbolized a reality of American politics: the most crucial decisions were made away from public scrutiny, in settings where cigar smoke curled around quiet negotiations.

The "smoke-filled room" was not a single place, but an enduring institution of power. Throughout the 20th century, this tradition persisted in Senate cloakrooms, private clubs, and exclusive lounges—spaces where legislation was not debated but designed, where alliances were forged, and where the machinery of governance moved forward without the glare of cameras or the voice of the electorate.

Even in global affairs, cigars became tools of quiet diplomacy. During the Cold War, meetings between Soviet and American officials often included the exchange of premium cigars—gestures that carried unspoken meanings of respect, rivalry, or negotiation. A well-selected cigar could serve as an icebreaker or a power move, symbolizing the shared understanding that, beyond ideology, there was an elite culture that transcended political divisions.

The smoke-filled room represented a paradox of American democracy. It was both a space of exclusion and a necessary stage for compromise, a setting where political transparency was sacrificed in favor of backroom dealmaking. For some, it was the shadowy side of politics, where elites subverted democratic ideals. For others, it was the pragmatic heart of governance, where unscripted, candid discussions allowed for real problem-solving outside the spectacle of public debate.

As the decades passed, public political discourse became more transparent, but the spirit of the smoke-filled room endured. Exclusive fundraisers, high-dollar donor meetings, and closed-door strategy sessions carried on the tradition—proving that while the physical smoke may have faded, the essence of backroom politics remained as potent as ever.

The Blackstone Hotel's infamous suite was more than a historical footnote—it was a revelation of the hidden gears of democracy, where the future of the country was shaped not by public mandate, but by the quiet negotiations of men with cigars in hand.

Cigars & The White House: The Presidential Smoke Signal

The presidency of the United States has always been more than a political office—it is a carefully constructed performance of power, authority, and national identity. For much of American history, the cigar has been an essential prop in this performance, a symbol of strength, diplomacy, and influence.

Presidential Archetypes: Smoke and Power

Long before cigars became a defining accessory of the presidency, James Madison (1809–1817) helped lay the foundation for tobacco's role in political culture. As a Virginia plantation owner, Madison was deeply tied to the economics of tobacco and was among the first presidents to embrace cigars—then commonly called "seegars." His enjoyment of cigars signaled a cultural shift from traditional pipe smoking to a more modern, refined form of tobacco consumption.

Ulysses S. Grant (1869–1877) would later embody the earliest archetype of presidential cigar culture. A Civil War hero with a widely publicized 20-a-day habit, Grant transformed the cigar from a personal indulgence into a national symbol. His ever-present cigars became synonymous with his battlefield resilience and political leadership. During cabinet meetings, Grant often used his cigars as a form of nonverbal communication—puffing calmly in deep thought or aggressively biting down when tensions ran high.

Theodore Roosevelt (1901–1909) elevated presidential cigar smoking to a tool of masculine performance. His habit reflected his larger-than-life persona, blending ruggedness with sophistication. Roosevelt famously used cigars as part of his diplomatic strategy, employing them in political negotiations much like he did his energetic handshakes and boisterous storytelling.

In contrast, Calvin Coolidge (1923–1929) represented a quieter, more introspective approach to cigar smoking. His long, mild cigars reflected his reserved nature, transforming the act of smoking into a meditative ritual rather than a theatrical display. Coolidge's cigars were not about dominance or diplomacy, but about personal discipline and quiet reflection.

Diplomatic Smoke: The White House as a Stage for Negotiation

For much of American history, the White House smoking room functioned as an unofficial diplomatic hub. Here, world leaders, political allies, and advisors gathered to discuss matters of war and peace, often over fine cigars. The ritual of sharing a cigar created an environment of camaraderie, where formalities could give way to candid conversation.

During World War II, Franklin D. Roosevelt (1933–1945) and Winston Churchill solidified their alliance in meetings that often stretched late into the night, their discussions accompanied by a steady haze of cigar smoke. Churchill later recalled that some of the war's most crucial decisions were made "through a veil of Cuban smoke." The shared tobacco ritual between the two leaders reinforced their personal bond, helping to strengthen the Allied partnership.

John F. Kennedy (1961–1963) represented the height of the cigar's symbolic power in American politics. His appreciation for fine cigars was no secret, though he carefully managed his public image in the new television era. While rarely photographed smoking, Kennedy's cigars became an unspoken symbol of his sophistication and global awareness. As we shall later see, the infamous moment when he stockpiled 1,200 Cuban cigars just before signing the Cuban trade embargo in 1962 demonstrated the deep entanglement of cigars with geopolitics.

The Twilight of Presidential Tobacco

Richard Nixon (1969–1974) marked the end of public cigar smoking in the White House. While he enjoyed cigars privately, cultural shifts were making tobacco use less acceptable in public life. Nixon's smoking habits reflected both his political calculation and personal anxieties—during the height of the Watergate scandal, aides recalled him chain-smoking cigars in moments of deep stress. Unlike his predecessors, who had used cigars to project strength, Nixon's reliance on them became more of a personal coping mechanism.

Ronald Reagan (1981–1989) signaled a cultural shift in presidential cigar smoking. He did not smoke cigars himself, understanding that shifting public perceptions made visible tobacco use a liability. He did, however, maintain a personal appreciation for the cigar as an object of prestige and was known to gift high-quality boxes to political allies and foreign dignitaries. His approach reflected the changing times—where cigars remained a symbol of prestige but were increasingly kept out of the public eye.

George H.W. Bush (1989–1993) continued this transition. While known to enjoy cigars privately, he kept his indulgence discreet, storing a well-maintained humidor in the White House residence rather than making smoking a visible part of his public persona.

Bill Clinton (1993–2001) briefly revived public attention to cigars, though not for traditional reasons—his use of a cigar in an infamous Oval Office scandal only reinforced how dramatically the cultural landscape around tobacco had changed.

By the time of George W. Bush (2001–2009) and Barack Obama (2009–2017), the tradition of presidential cigar smoking had largely faded. Though some presidents, including Obama, were known to have smoked cigarettes, the once-prevalent image of a cigar-smoking commander-in-chief had all but disappeared.

The Legacy of Smoke

For generations of American leaders, cigars were more than a personal indulgence—they were tools of diplomacy, symbols of authority, and extensions of their public personas. Whether used as a form of negotiation, a mark of resilience, or a subtle expression of power, the cigar played a unique role in shaping the presidency.

As smoking became less socially acceptable, the presidential cigar became a relic of an earlier era. Yet, in private cigar lounges and exclusive gatherings, the ritual remains—quietly carrying on a tradition that once defined the highest office in the land.

The Decline of Public Cigar Culture: Power's Quiet Retreat

The transformation of the cigar from a widely accepted symbol of political power to a more private indulgence was not a sudden collapse but a gradual shift influenced by evolving social norms, public health awareness, and cultural changes.

By the 1980s, the once-prominent image of political leaders smoking cigars in public had largely faded. The White House, which had once been a center of cigar-fueled diplomacy, was undergoing a cultural transformation. Public smoking restrictions expanded across government buildings, workplaces, and social venues, systematically dismantling the infrastructure of cigar culture in political spaces.

The Erosion of the Smoking Room

For much of American history, political negotiations and high-level discussions took place in the haze of cigar smoke. From congressional backrooms to private club lounges, tobacco was part of the atmosphere in which power was exercised. However, as public sentiment toward smoking shifted, these spaces began to change.

In the late 20th century, federal buildings became battlegrounds for new smoking regulations. As anti-smoking campaigns gained traction, restrictions spread from hospitals and schools to courthouses and legislative chambers. Political figures who had once been photographed confidently smoking cigars in public now had to carefully manage their image, aware that a simple photo could generate negative publicity.

By the 1990s, smoking bans had transformed the political and corporate landscape. Lawmakers, lobbyists, and business executives who once networked over cigars in public lounges now retreated to more private settings. The cigar remained a powerful tool for building relationships and sealing deals, but it was no longer a public spectacle.

The Cultural Shift: From Status Symbol to Social Liability

As medical research continued to highlight the health risks of smoking, the perception of cigars evolved. What had once been a marker of sophistication and authority was increasingly viewed as a vice. The 1964 U.S. Surgeon General's report on smoking and health had already set the stage for change, and by the 1980s and 1990s, the anti-smoking movement was a dominant force in public policy.

Public figures began distancing themselves from visible tobacco use. Politicians who had once embraced cigar culture now found themselves adjusting to a world where smoking was seen as outdated or even irresponsible. While cigars retained their allure among private circles, their presence in public life diminished.

Even in the business world, where cigars had long been associated with success, attitudes shifted. Corporate America began prioritizing health-conscious workplace policies, and many executives who once conducted meetings over cigars adapted to a new reality. The decline of smoke-filled boardrooms mirrored the changes happening in political spaces.

The Persistence of Private Cigar Culture

Despite the decline of public cigar smoking, the tradition never disappeared—it simply moved behind closed doors. Elite clubs, invitation-only fundraisers, and high-level diplomatic meetings continued to embrace cigars as part of an exclusive social ritual.

In these private settings, the cigar remained a silent marker of influence. While political leaders no longer smoked openly in government offices, they could still be found enjoying cigars in private residences, luxury hotels, and members-only lounges. The ritual of lighting a fine cigar and engaging in candid conversation remained a powerful tool in business and politics, even as its public visibility declined.

The decline of public cigar culture did not signify the end of its role in political and business power structures. Rather, it marked an adaptation to changing societal norms. The cigar's presence in public life may have faded, but its influence persisted in more discreet forms.

While the days of cigar-smoking presidents and smoke-filled congressional chambers are gone, the cigar has remained a quiet symbol of status and influence. In exclusive clubs, behind closed doors, and in the moments between official meetings, cigars continue to serve as instruments of networking, negotiation, and tradition.

The cultural retreat of cigars from public spaces reflects broader shifts in American society, but as history has shown, power and tradition have a way of enduring—even if only in whispers of smoke behind the scenes.

WHAT DID THEY SMOKE?

The Cigars of Political Power

Not all cigars were created equal in the world of political influence. Some brands became synonymous with power, prestige, and diplomacy, carefully chosen by leaders as a reflection of their status and preferences. The cigars smoked by presidents, diplomats, and influential figures were more than just tobacco—they were symbols of authority, tools of negotiation, and markers of personal style.

Presidential Preferences

James Madison, as a Virginia plantation owner deeply tied to tobacco cultivation, likely enjoyed locally grown cigars. While historical records provide little detail on his preferences, it is reasonable to assume his cigars were hand-rolled from American-grown leaves, a quiet nod to the nation's emerging economic independence.

Ulysses S. Grant, a battle-hardened Civil War general, preferred strong Cuban cigars. His 20-a-day habit was less about indulgence and more about endurance. Smoking became part of his identity, a ritual that accompanied him from the battlefield to the White House. His fondness for cigars was so well known that admirers sent him thousands as gifts, reinforcing the image of a leader who never wavered, even under pressure.

Theodore Roosevelt exclusively smoked Cuban-made Punch cigars, a fitting choice for a man known for his blend of rugged masculinity and international sophistication. His cigars were not merely personal luxuries but also political tools. He often used them to establish camaraderie in negotiations and to reinforce his carefully curated image of bold, unshakable leadership.

John F. Kennedy's relationship with cigars was both personal and geopolitical. His preference was for H. Upmann Petit Coronas—a preference whose consequences would echo through the embargo of 1962, as Chapter 4 will detail.

Ronald Reagan, by contrast, did not smoke cigars. He was, however, a frequent gifter of premium cigars to political allies and foreign dignitaries— a tradition consistent with the cigar's continuing role as a marker of prestige even as it disappeared from the president's own hand.

Cigars as Diplomatic Tools

Beyond personal preference, cigars often played a role in diplomacy. During the Cold War, Cuban cigars became more than just luxury items—they were unspoken gestures of respect and negotiation. While the U.S. embargo prevented their legal sale in America, Cuban cigars remained a prized gift among world leaders. Offering a rare or high-quality cigar could serve as a diplomatic icebreaker, signaling goodwill and fostering informal moments of connection.

One of the most coveted cigars in political circles was the Cohiba, a brand originally produced exclusively for Fidel Castro's personal use. Each cigar was meticulously handcrafted, designed not just for quality but as a statement of revolutionary prestige. Over time, Cohibas became sought-after status symbols among global political elites, reinforcing the link between cigars and power.

Brands of Influence

Certain cigars transcended mere consumption to become symbols of authority. The H. Upmann brand, founded by German bankers in Havana in 1844, became synonymous with business and political elites. Montecristo cigars—named after Alexandre Dumas' famous novel—represented a carefully curated experience of exclusivity and refinement, favored by those who wished to project an image of sophistication.

Winston Churchill's loyalty to Romeo y Julieta cigars cemented the brand's reputation as a statesman's choice. His famous habit of keeping a lit cigar throughout meetings, speeches, and even moments of crisis reinforced the association between cigars and resilience under pressure. The Churchill-sized cigar, named in his honor, remains one of the most recognizable cigar formats to this day.

The Political Economy of Tobacco

By the mid-20th century, cigars had evolved into powerful political artifacts, no longer just indulgences but essential instruments of status, negotiation, and authority. A premium cigar could cost the equivalent of a day's wage for the average worker, but for political elites, price was irrelevant. What mattered was the message it conveyed—a declaration of influence, wealth, and belonging to an exclusive inner circle.

The cigar had become a performative tool in political theater. In the halls of Congress and the corridors of power, the way a politician selected, cut, and lit a cigar was as carefully considered as the phrasing of a speech or the delivery of a handshake. Every detail—the brand, country of origin, size, and smoking style—was an unspoken but deliberate statement, a quiet assertion of cultural, economic, or geopolitical alignment.

But cigars weren't just symbols of domestic political power; they were also tools of global diplomacy. If a well-chosen cigar could establish authority in a political chamber, it could also serve as an unspoken gesture of goodwill across negotiating tables.

Cigars in International Diplomacy: Tobacco as a Global Language

Diplomacy has always been more art than science, and cigars emerged as one of its most nuanced instruments. They were not merely smoking products but carefully choreographed tools of international communication—silent negotiators that spoke volumes without uttering a word.

During the Cold War, Cuban cigars became extraordinary diplomatic artifacts. When Soviet and American diplomats exchanged these carefully selected tobacco rolls, they were doing far more than sharing a smoke. Each cigar represented a potential bridge across ideological divides, a momentary softening of geopolitical tensions.

The Cuban Missile Crisis (1962) provided a fascinating backdrop to this tobacco diplomacy. While official negotiations happened in sterile rooms, informal exchanges of premium cigars helped create subtle channels of communication. Diplomats understood that a shared Cohiba could convey more goodwill than countless formal communiqués.

In Latin American negotiations, cigars functioned as cultural passports. A diplomat's knowledge of tobacco—its origins, rolling techniques, and regional variations—could establish credibility faster than any formal credentials. Understanding the difference between a Nicaraguan and a Cuban tobacco blend became a form of diplomatic fluency.

During international summits, cigars became ritualistic objects of soft power. Leaders like Fidel Castro used tobacco as a form of cultural projection, transforming a simple agricultural product into a symbol of national identity and defiance. A Cuban cigar was never just a cigar—it was a statement of sovereignty.

British and American diplomats in the Caribbean often used cigars as subtle negotiation tools. Trade agreements, colonial discussions, and economic treaties were frequently preceded or accompanied by carefully selected tobacco exchanges. The act of lighting and sharing a cigar created a momentary space of potential understanding, where personal rapport could be established before formal agreements were reached.

By the late 20th century, cigars had become sophisticated instruments of international communication. They represented a language beyond words—a diplomatic dialect that spoke of respect, tradition, and the potential for collaboration.

Although cigars played a role in domestic political rituals, their influence extended far beyond national borders. They became an integral part of international diplomacy, creating moments of connection in even the most strained negotiations.

One such moment stands out—a striking example of how cigars could serve as both a diplomatic bridge and a quiet act of defiance. The next section, "A Diplomatic Cigar Moment: Tito's Defiant Smoke & A White House Moment," captures this dynamic in action.

A Diplomatic Cigar Moment: Tito's Defiant Smoke & A White House Moment

When Yugoslav President Josip Broz Tito visited the White House during the Nixon administration, in October 1971, he achieved a unique diplomatic distinction: he became arguably the only foreign leader to openly smoke a Cuban cigar in the White House during the Cuban Embargo period—and did so sitting right next to President Nixon.

The moment was remarkable not just for its audacity, but for its geopolitical complexity. Despite the U.S. trade embargo against Cuba, Tito brazenly lit up a Cuban cigar, a direct violation of the diplomatic and economic restrictions then in place. Nixon, known for his own cigar appreciation, did not object.

This small act of tobacco diplomacy symbolized the intricate dance of Cold War international relations. Tito, a non-aligned leader who maintained a delicate balance between the Soviet and Western blocs, seemed to deliberately challenge the embargo's strictures. By smoking a Cuban cigar in the heart of American political power, he made a subtle but pointed statement about the arbitrary nature of Cold War restrictions.

Nixon, R. (1971). Meeting with President Josip Broz Tito. Nixon Presidential Library.

The incident went largely unreported at the time, becoming a fascinating footnote in the complex history of presidential cigar culture—a moment where a single lit cigar spoke volumes about international power dynamics.

Tobacco, Wealth, and Political Influence: The Economics of Smoke

The tobacco industry was never merely a commercial enterprise; it was a powerful political force that shaped American democracy through strategic lobbying, campaign financing, and deep political relationships.

By the early 20th century, tobacco companies had perfected the art of political influence. The American Tobacco Company and its successors did not just sell cigarettes and cigars—they purchased access to lawmakers. Congressional committees, state legislatures, and federal agencies were systematically cultivated through a combination of campaign contributions, strategic networking, and carefully managed relationships.

Lobbying became an essential tool for the industry. Tobacco representatives did not merely argue for their economic interests; they positioned tobacco as a pillar of American tradition. They framed restrictions on the industry as attacks on personal freedom, agricultural livelihoods, and state economies. Each legislative session saw tobacco lobbyists working to protect their interests, using both financial influence and well-crafted public relations campaigns.

Campaign financing became the industry's most potent weapon. From local elections to presidential races, tobacco money flowed through the veins of the American political system. Southern states, where tobacco farming was vital to the economy, became strongholds of industry-backed political power. Candidates who aligned with the industry's interests were generously funded, while those who supported anti-smoking measures often faced well-financed opposition.

The financial scale of tobacco's political influence was immense. Before significant regulation, tobacco companies could contribute millions to campaigns and lobbying efforts, creating a vast network of political allies. Lawmakers from tobacco-producing states were not just representatives of their constituents—they were defenders of an industry that provided jobs, tax revenue, and international trade value.

By the 1960s, as health concerns surrounding tobacco grew, the industry shifted from aggressive expansion to strategic defense. Lobbyists worked to challenge emerging medical research, delay regulatory measures, and promote alternative narratives about smoking. They invested heavily in scientific studies designed to cast doubt on the link between smoking and disease, funding experts who would testify in congressional hearings and public forums.

The tobacco industry's political influence remained formidable even as public sentiment shifted. It resisted regulation for decades, ensuring that warning labels, advertising restrictions, and smoking bans took years to implement. When new policies threatened profits, the industry responded with lawsuits, media campaigns, and financial contributions to politicians willing to push back against restrictions.

The story of tobacco in American politics was never just about a product—it was about power. The industry's ability to shape legislation, influence public perception, and maintain political relevance, even in the face of overwhelming scientific evidence, demonstrated the deep entanglement of economic interests and governance.

Even as smoking declined in popularity, the political strategies developed by the tobacco industry set a precedent for corporate influence in government. The tactics honed by tobacco executives—lobbying, campaign financing, and public messaging—would later be adopted by industries ranging from pharmaceuticals to fossil fuels.

Conclusion: The Enduring Ritual of Power

The cigar's journey through American political culture is a testament to the subtle languages of power. What began as a public ritual of influence has transformed into a nuanced, carefully choreographed performance of connection and negotiation.

Smoke may have cleared from the visible spaces of political deal-making, but the essence of the cigar's cultural significance remains. Modern political fundraisers, exclusive club gatherings, and high-level diplomatic exchanges continue to whisper the old language: a dialect of tobacco understood by everyone in the room.

Each cigar now carries the weight of historical memory. It is simultaneously an artifact and a living symbol—a bridge between past and present, between the open performances of political power and its more discreet contemporary manifestations. The contemporary cigar represents continuity, a small rolled testament to the evolving nature of American political culture.

In the quiet, wood-paneled rooms of power—private clubs, discreet lounges, exclusive gatherings—the tradition endures. The cigar remains what it has always been: a tool of connection, a marker of influence, a silent narrator of political narratives.

The story of the cigar in American politics is far from over. It has simply entered a new, more subtle chapter of its complex historical performance—a performance about to encounter its most dramatic act of transformation.

Before we dive into the next chapter, let's take a 'visual break' with some vintage advertising.

Visual Break: Iconic Cigar Ads of the Early 1900s

Cigars have long been symbols of refinement, status, and leisure, but their perception was carefully crafted through advertising. In the early 20th century, brands embraced bold, creative, and sometimes controversial marketing strategies to shape consumer desire and establish cigars as a staple of sophistication.

From the booming cigar industry of Tampa to the rise of mass-market branding and aspirational imagery, these advertisements did more than sell a product—they helped define an era. They captured the craftsmanship, prestige, and indulgence that made cigars a powerful cultural symbol during their golden age.

"Imported Havana Cigars" advertisement, Life Magazine, 1928. This ad urges consumers to look for the official seal of authenticity, ensuring they receive genuine Cuban cigars in a market flooded with counterfeits. During Prohibition (1920–1933), high demand and widespread smuggling—possibly involving figures like Al Capone—fueled concerns over fraudulent cigars. The advertisement reflects efforts to protect the reputation of premium Cuban cigars by educating buyers on how to verify authenticity.

"Ten Years The Standard" advertising sign, Cremo Cigars, early 1900s. Unlike competitors that marketed cigars as a masculine indulgence, Cremo Cigars deliberately featured women in its advertising to make cigars appear more modern, refined, and socially acceptable. These ads often depicted elegant women presenting Cremo cigars approvingly, reinforcing their status as a sophisticated, everyday pleasure. By associating cigars with femininity and charm—rather than just power or wealth—Cremo broadened its appeal in an industry dominated by male-focused branding.

"A Perfect Smoke" advertisement, Robert Burns Cigars, 1910s–1920s. Robert Burns Cigars blended tradition with modernity, using imagery of an airplane and stylish figures to convey both heritage and progress. By linking cigars to cutting-edge technology, the brand appealed to men who valued elegance and adventure. This balance of refinement and innovation exemplified how cigar brands of the era sought to stand out—offering a "perfect smoke" that embodied both leisure and modern sophistication.

Plantista Cigars advertisement, Compeer Cigar Co., Indianapolis, early 1900s. This ad reflects the era's luxury-driven tobacco marketing, featuring a well-dressed gentleman to evoke status and refinement. With its vibrant colors and ornate design, it served as a striking point-of-sale display, ensuring visibility in retail settings. At a time when cigars symbolized prestige, such advertisements played a key role in shaping brand identity and attracting discerning smokers.

"Are your nerves like this? The Girard Cigar never gets on your nerves" (1919) Girard Cigars. In 1919, Girard Cigars launched an advertising campaign emphasizing the health benefits of their mild cigars. One notable advertisement featured the headline, "Are your nerves like this?" and depicted a man appearing agitated. The ad suggested that smoking Girard Cigars could alleviate nervousness without adverse effects, stating, "The Girard is famous for the fact that it never gets on your nerves. Doctors recommend it, and smoke it, too." This approach aimed to position Girard Cigars as a soothing choice endorsed by medical professionals, appealing to consumers concerned about the health implications of smoking.

CHAPTER 4

The Cuban Embargo:
A Defining Disruption

Cold War Tensions | A cigar is more than a luxury—it is a link to history, trade, and power. The early 20th century saw Cuba emerge as an economic powerhouse, deeply tied to the United States through its sugar, tobacco, and tourism industries. American investment poured into Cuba, and Cuban cigars became a symbol of prestige among U.S. elites. However, a series of global economic and political crises would soon unravel these close ties.

The Great Depression and the Decline of the Cigar Market (1929–1939)

The Great Depression (1929–1939) devastated global economies, and Cuba was no exception. The dramatic drop in consumer spending in the United States led to a sharp decline in demand for luxury goods, including premium cigars. The Smoot-Hawley Tariff Act (1930) further exacerbated the crisis by imposing steep import duties on foreign goods, making Cuban cigars prohibitively expensive for American consumers.

As sales plummeted, many small cigar manufacturers closed, while others turned to mechanization to cut costs. This shift threatened Cuba's tradition of hand-rolled cigars, as cheaper, machine-made domestic alternatives gained popularity. The industry's downturn also deepened public discontent with Cuba's U.S.-backed government, laying the groundwork for future political unrest.

World War II and the Role of Cigars (1939–1945)

During World War II (1939–1945), cigars remained deeply ingrained in military culture. The U.S. military included them in rations for officers and enlisted men, reinforcing their association with leadership and camaraderie. Meanwhile, British Prime Minister Winston Churchill, famous for his ever-present Cuban cigars, became a global symbol of resilience, keeping Cuban cigars in the public eye even as wartime rationing limited supply.

Trade restrictions and high tariffs, first imposed during the Great Depression, remained in effect throughout the war, further limiting access to Cuban cigars in the United States. As supply dwindled, the black market flourished, turning Cuban cigars into a rare wartime luxury. Their scarcity only increased their desirability, solidifying their status as a prized commodity despite ongoing geopolitical tensions.

The Post-War Economic Boom and the Golden Age of Cuban Cigars (1945–1959)

After World War II, the United States entered an era of extraordinary prosperity. Rising incomes, suburban expansion, and the emergence of corporate culture fueled demand for luxury goods—including cigars. This post-war economic boom reshaped consumer habits, making fine cigars a staple of social gatherings, business meetings, and private leisure.

During this period, Havana's renowned tobacco solidified its status as the world's finest. By the 1950s, premium Cuban tobacco accounted for nearly half of all premium cigars sold in the United States, an unmatched market dominance. Smoking a Cuban cigar was not just an indulgence; it was a sign of refinement, a marker of success that crossed social classes. From blue-collar workers relaxing after a long day to high-powered executives sealing business deals, the presence of a fine Havana cigar carried meaning beyond its smoke.

Cuba's economy thrived under this trade relationship. Alongside sugar, tobacco was one of the island's most valuable exports, supporting thousands of workers in farming, processing, and manufacturing. Cuban cigar brands such as Montecristo, Partagás, and Romeo y Julieta became household names in the U.S., celebrated for their consistency and craftsmanship. The legendary Vuelta Abajo region, often called "Cuba's green gold triangle," produced the richest and most complex tobacco in the world. This small western province was uniquely suited for growing all three major components of a cigar—wrappers, fillers, and binders—creating a level of quality that no other region could match.

Beyond Cuba, the cigar trade extended into major U.S. manufacturing hubs. Cities like Tampa's Ybor City and New York, along with Pennsylvania's cigar-producing regions, relied on Cuban leaf to produce premium cigars for American consumers. Tampa, in particular, had become a center of innovation, with Cuban and Spanish immigrant cigar makers developing new techniques to use Havana tobacco while navigating U.S. import tariffs. By the 1950s the industry was already in decline — but the surviving factories still produced cigars in volumes that made Tampa a major U.S. tobacco hub. Skilled rollers, known as torcedores, crafted cigars by hand in workshops where storytelling, news discussions, and even live newspaper readings became part of the daily routine.

For decades, Havana's tobacco had been the undisputed gold standard. Cuban cigars were synonymous with quality, their popularity extending from small-town cigar lounges to the most elite social circles. They were featured in Hollywood films, enjoyed by statesmen, and written about in lifestyle magazines that positioned them as the epitome of sophistication. This was an era when enjoying a fine cigar was as much a ritual as it was a pastime.

Yet, beneath this prosperity, social and political tensions in Cuba were intensifying. The nation's economic structure was highly dependent on U.S. trade, and many of its industries—cigars included—were backed by American investors. However, Cuban workers saw little of the wealth their labor generated, and dissatisfaction was growing. Corruption, economic inequality, and frustration with foreign influence fueled unrest, setting the stage for revolution.

By the late 1950s, the golden age of Cuban cigars in the U.S. was on the verge of collapse. The rise of Fidel Castro and his radical economic policies would soon disrupt one of the most profitable cigar markets in the world, leading to a crisis that would reshape the global tobacco industry forever.

The Rise of Castro and the Shift Toward Communism (1959–1961)

In 1959, Fidel Castro led a revolution that upended Cuba's economic and political order, severing its long-standing ties with the United States. He nationalized industries—including American-owned businesses and cigar factories—without compensation, sending shockwaves through the U.S. economy.

As Castro aligned with the Soviet Union, Cold War tensions escalated. The failed Bay of Pigs invasion (1961), a CIA-backed attempt to overthrow Castro, only pushed Cuba deeper into the Soviet sphere.

As a communist regime took hold just 90 miles from Florida, the U.S. viewed Cuba as both an economic and ideological threat. In response, President John F. Kennedy prepared to implement a comprehensive trade embargo—one that would forever change the cigar industry.

The Last Night of Legal Cuban Cigars and the Immediate Fallout

On the evening of February 6, 1962, White House Press Secretary Pierre Salinger received an urgent call from President John F. Kennedy. The request was precise and unusually time-sensitive:

"Pierre, I need a favor. Get me Cuban cigars—at least a thousand of them. And I need them by tomorrow morning."

The urgency in Kennedy's voice suggested this was more than a simple indulgence. Just days earlier, on February 3, he had quietly signed Proclamation 3447, authorizing a full trade embargo against Cuba. However, the announcement had not yet been made public, and the restrictions would not take effect until February 7—leaving a brief window of opportunity.

By dawn, Salinger had reportedly secured 1,200 H. Upmann Petit Coronas—Kennedy's favored brand. According to Salinger's later account, only after ensuring his personal supply was stocked did the President allow the embargo to take full effect.

With the stroke of a pen, the world's most celebrated cigars vanished from American shelves.

The announcement sent shockwaves through the cigar-smoking community. In lounges from Manhattan to San Francisco, the atmosphere was electric with disbelief and urgency. Wealthy collectors and casual smokers alike understood that an era was ending. Retailers conducted frantic inventory checks, knowing that every remaining Cuban cigar in their humidors was now a collector's item. Overnight, prices surged—a Montecristo that once cost $5 suddenly became a $50 treasure, as speculators fought for every last box.

For U.S. cigar manufacturers, the embargo represented an existential crisis. Cities like Tampa's Ybor City, long reliant on Cuban leaf, were particularly devastated. The embargo disrupted generations-old trade routes, supplier relationships, and blending techniques, forcing manufacturers to seek alternatives.

The U.S. cigar industry scrambled to adjust. Cigar makers became improvisational artists, experimenting with tobacco from Nicaragua, Honduras, and the Dominican Republic. Some saw this as an impossible challenge; others viewed it as an opportunity for reinvention.

The timeline below provides a sequential overview of the key shifts in the U.S. cigar market from the pre-embargo era through the following three decades.

TIMELINE: The Transformation of the American Cigar Industry, 1959-1990

1959: The Cuban Revolution Begins
- Castro seizes power
- Nationalization of the tobacco industry starts
- First tremors of a coming economic earthquake

1962: The Embargo's Hammer Falls
- U.S. completely bans Cuban tobacco imports
- 90% of Cuba's tobacco exports vanish
- $27 million in annual Cuban tobacco imports vanish; $4 million of that in premium cigars

1970s: The Global Tobacco Diaspora
- Padrón family establishes operations in Nicaragua
- Dominican Republic emerges as a new tobacco powerhouse
- Honduras begins its tobacco transformation

1980s: The Age of Innovation
- Early hybrid tobacco strains emerged in the 1960s and 1970s, with expanded development and experimentation accelerating in the 1980s.
- Advanced fermentation techniques emerge
- Multi-origin blending becomes an art form

1990s: The Cigar Renaissance
- Cigar Aficionado magazine launches
- Boutique brands proliferate
- Premium cigar market explodes

A Comparative Snapshot:
Pre-Embargo (1950s)
- Cuban cigars: 75% of U.S. premium market
- Annual production: ~250 million cigars
- Centralized, traditional production model

Post-Embargo (1990)
- Nicaragua/Dominican Republic dominate
- Annual production: ~500 million cigars
- Diverse, innovative, globally distributed production.

"I Want You For The Diplomat Corps!" (1967) – White Owl Cigars. With Cuban cigars banned from the U.S. market after 1962, American brands needed to reposition themselves. This 1967 White Owl ad cleverly played on Cold War diplomacy, portraying a cigar-smoking "recruiter" encouraging Americans to join the "Diplomat Corps"—a humorous nod to the fact that Cuban cigars were now off-limits. This ad exemplifies how domestic cigar brands adapted, using wit and patriotism to maintain their relevance in a rapidly changing industry.

Yet, while the legal market struggled to reinvent itself, another side of the cigar trade was thriving. A booming black market emerged, turning Cuban cigars into a coveted contraband, much like Prohibition-era liquor.

Smuggling networks capitalized on their scarcity, driving prices to extraordinary heights, with a single pre-embargo box fetching thousands of dollars.

Collectors treated Cuban cigars like rare art pieces. Sealed boxes from before the embargo became prized possessions, their value increasing with each passing year. Wealthy enthusiasts displayed their collections like fine art, while museums and private collectors began treating these cigars as historical artifacts, their significance transcending mere tobacco.

The embargo's economic impact was both immediate and far-reaching.

In 1960, the United States imported approximately $27 million in Cuban tobacco, including over $4 million in premium cigars—a trade that vanished overnight. While this represented less than 0.2 percent of total U.S. imports, it was Cuba's largest dollar-earning agricultural export, with 95 percent of its U.S. farm exports coming from tobacco in 1961.

Yet the cultural shift was even more profound. What had once been a simple indulgence—smoking a Cuban cigar—became a politically charged act. Lighting a Partagás, Montecristo, or H. Upmann was no longer just about personal enjoyment; it now carried symbolic weight, transforming a private ritual into a statement on Cold War geopolitics.

As the dust settled, one profound truth emerged: the global cigar industry had been fundamentally transformed. The Cuban Embargo was far more than a political restriction—it was a seismic event that permanently reshaped how the world understood, produced, and consumed premium tobacco.

The Global Cigar Renaissance: A New Industry in Exile

While Cuba struggled under the weight of its severed trade relationship with the U.S., its most skilled cigar makers were seeking new opportunities abroad. The embargo unintentionally ignited a rebirth—what had once been a Cuba-centric industry was now dispersing across the globe, leading to the rise of new cigar-making powerhouses.

In the wake of the embargo, Nicaragua, the Dominican Republic, and Honduras rapidly rose to prominence. Exiled Cuban cigar makers, unwilling to work under Castro's nationalized industry, brought their generational expertise to new lands. They planted Cuban-seed tobacco, adapted blending techniques, and established factories that would eventually compete with, and even surpass, Cuba's cigar legacy.

The Ybor City district of Tampa, which had once been the center of Cuban-American cigar production, adapted to the changing landscape. Manufacturers who had long relied on Cuban leaf now turned to alternative sources, crafting blends that preserved the art of traditional cigar rolling.

By the late 1960s, these exile-led factories were no longer just surviving—they were thriving. The embargo, meant to cripple Cuban cigars, had inadvertently fueled a global renaissance of tobacco craftsmanship.

A New Era of Innovation and Reinvention

Without access to Cuban tobacco, cigar makers were forced to innovate. They experimented with:

- New tobacco-growing regions, including Nicaragua's Estelí Valley and the Dominican Republic's Cibao Valley.
- Advanced fermentation techniques to recreate the depth and complexity of Cuban cigars.
- Hybrid tobacco strains that mimicked the qualities of Cuban-seed tobacco while adapting to new climates.

Cigar-making was no longer about replicating Cuban cigars—it was about creating something entirely new. Brands like Padrón (Nicaragua) and Arturo Fuente (Dominican Republic) embraced multi-origin blending, turning a crisis into an opportunity for reinvention.

As the 1970s and 1980s progressed, these non-Cuban cigars gained international acclaim. By the 1990s, the premium cigar market was booming, fueled by a resurgence of interest in handmade cigars, the rise of luxury cigar lounges, and the launch of *Cigar Aficionado* magazine, which helped shape modern cigar culture.

The Cuban embargo, intended as a punitive measure, had instead sparked a technological and artistic renaissance in the cigar world. It forced innovation, celebrated diversity, and proved that true craftsmanship knows no national boundaries.

By the turn of the century, the dominance of Cuban cigars was no longer absolute. The exile-led industry had redefined what it meant to create a premium cigar. What emerged was no longer a Cuban cigar in exile. It was something new.

Rebuilding an Industry from Exile

When the Cuban trade embargo severed the primary artery of global premium tobacco, it triggered a remarkable diaspora of cigar expertise. This was not merely a commercial disruption, but a complex human story of survival, innovation, and cultural preservation. Exiled Cuban cigar makers carried with them generations of knowledge—secret blending techniques, intimate understanding of tobacco cultivation, and an unwavering commitment to craftsmanship that would transform the global tobacco landscape.

Nicaragua: The Volcanic Frontier of Tobacco Reinvention

The story of Nicaraguan tobacco is a testament to human resilience and geographical serendipity. When Cuban cigar makers began arriving in Nicaragua in the late 1960s and early 1970s, they discovered a landscape that seemed almost divinely designed for tobacco cultivation. The volcanic regions of Estelí and Jalapa bore an uncanny resemblance to Cuba's legendary Vuelta Abajo—rich, mineral-laden soils that seemed to whisper promises of exceptional tobacco.

José Orlando Padrón's journey epitomizes this remarkable transformation. After leaving Cuba in 1961 and spending time in Madrid and New York, he arrived in Miami with little more than determination and generational tobacco knowledge. Working initially as a carpenter to fund his dream, Padrón would eventually establish a cigar empire in Miami before moving production to Nicaragua in 1970—an empire that would become synonymous with quality and stubbornness in equal measure.

The volcanic terroir of Nicaragua became more than a geographical feature—it became a narrative of rebirth. Tobacco farmers who had lost everything in Cuba found not just a new homeland, but a canvas for reinvention. The Estelí region, with its unique microclimate and mineral-rich soils, began producing tobacco that wasn't just a replacement for Cuban leaf, but a distinct, powerful alternative.

By the 1980s, brands like Padrón had not just survived but were thriving. They weren't trying to imitate Cuban cigars—they were creating something entirely new. The Nicaraguan cigar became a symbol of transformation, each leaf telling a story of what survived the journey.

The Dominican Republic: From Agricultural Afterthought to Global Powerhouse

If Nicaragua was the passionate newcomer, the Dominican Republic was the strategic opportunist. When the Cuban market collapsed, the Dominican Republic positioned itself as the most sophisticated alternative. Carlos Fuente Sr. and Carlos Fuente Jr. of Arturo Fuente became architects of this transformation, turning the Dominican Republic into the world's premier cigar producer.

The Dominican success was no accident. It was a carefully orchestrated combination of ideal growing conditions, strategic marketing, and an understanding of what American consumers desired. Regions like the fertile Cibao Valley became new tobacco paradises, producing leaves that were simultaneously familiar and innovative.

Brands like Davidoff transformed the Dominican cigar from a mere product to a luxury experience. They understood that they weren't just selling tobacco—they were selling a lifestyle, a statement of sophistication. The Dominican cigar became a global ambassador, changing perceptions about what premium tobacco could represent.

Honduras: The Unexpected Champion

Honduras emerged as the quiet revolutionary of the post-embargo cigar world. While Nicaragua and the Dominican Republic garnered headlines, Honduran tobacco makers were diligently building a reputation for robust, earthy cigars that would develop a fiercely loyal following.

The Jamastran Valley, with its unique microclimate, became a crucible of innovation. Brands like Camacho didn't just produce cigars; they created bold, unapologetic tobacco experiences that challenged traditional flavor profiles. They were the rebels of the cigar world, proving that excellence could emerge from the most unexpected places.

By the 1990s, the global cigar market had been completely transformed. What had begun as a political disruption had become a global renaissance of tobacco craftsmanship. Cuban exiles hadn't just rebuilt an industry— they had reimagined it.

The embargo, intended as a punitive measure, had inadvertently created something extraordinary. It forced innovation, celebrated diversity, and proved that true craftsmanship knows no national boundaries. The global cigar market was no longer about a single nation's supremacy. It belonged to whoever could grow, blend, and roll well—wherever they happened to be.

The Great Tobacco Diaspora: The Embargo Reshapes a Global Industry

The Cuban trade embargo was more than a mere political maneuver—it was a human drama of epic proportions, a seismic event that would rewrite the global narrative of tobacco production. Imagine generations of farmers, craftsmen, and merchants suddenly stripped of their economic identity, their ancestral lands, and their most cherished traditions.

In the tobacco fields of Cuba, the impact was immediate and devastating. Families who had cultivated tobacco for centuries found themselves standing on land that no longer promised sustenance. The Vuelta Abajo region, once the beating heart of the world's finest tobacco production, became a landscape of economic uncertainty and personal heartbreak.

Statistical evidence tells a stark story of destruction. By 1962, a staggering 90 percent of Cuba's tobacco exports were destined for the United States. The embargo didn't just interrupt a trade route—it obliterated an entire economic ecosystem. Overnight, skilled torcedores found themselves economic refugees, their centuries-old craft suddenly rendered obsolete.

The global response was both unexpected and remarkable. Countries like Nicaragua and the Dominican Republic didn't just see an economic opportunity—they witnessed a cultural migration. Cuban tobacco expertise didn't vanish; it dispersed like seeds carried on the wind, taking root in new soils, adapting, and ultimately thriving.

Efforts by the Soviet bloc to sustain Cuba's tobacco industry proved noble yet ultimately futile. Communist countries lacked the sophisticated tobacco consumption culture of the United States. By 1970, Cuba was forced into a desperate economic pivot, restructuring agricultural exports to markets that could never truly appreciate the nuanced art of tobacco cultivation.

What emerged was a remarkable story of global reinvention. Tobacco farmers and cigar makers—once fierce competitors—found themselves united by a shared experience of displacement. They began experimenting, blending tobaccos from different regions, developing innovative growing techniques, and creating a more diverse and resilient global tobacco market.

The irony was profound. An embargo intended to isolate Cuba had the opposite effect. Cuban tobacco knowledge became a global currency. Techniques for growing, curing, and rolling cigars spread across Nicaragua, the Dominican Republic, Honduras, and beyond. What was meant to be a punishment became an unexpected form of cultural exportation.

By the late 1970s, the cigar world had been completely transformed. The monolithic Cuban tobacco industry had fragmented into a complex, dynamic global ecosystem. Small producers, once overshadowed by Cuban dominance, now found themselves at the forefront of innovation.

The human spirit of adaptation had triumphed. What began as a political restriction had inadvertently created a renaissance of tobacco craftsmanship —a testament to those who refused to be defined by political boundaries.

In the smoke of these new cigars, one could taste more than tobacco. One could taste hope, survival, and the unbreakable human capacity to reinvent oneself.

The embargo's impact extended far beyond mere trade restrictions. It triggered a technological and cultural revolution that would reshape how tobacco was grown, processed, and understood.

The Scientific Rebirth of an Ancient Craft

The Cuban Embargo forced the cigar industry into a period of unprecedented technological and agricultural innovation. Without access to Cuban tobacco, manufacturers had to reimagine the entire process of cultivation, curing, and blending—giving rise to a new era of scientific advancements in tobacco production.

Hybrid Tobacco Strains: Engineering the Future of Flavor

Agricultural scientists and master growers worked to develop hybrid tobacco strains that could replicate the complexity of Cuban tobacco while thriving in different climates. In Nicaragua, the Dominican Republic, and Honduras, experimental fields became living laboratories. Farmers meticulously studied soil composition, humidity levels, and temperature fluctuations, treating tobacco cultivation with the precision of scientific research.

The volcanic soils of Nicaragua's Estelí Valley and Honduras's Jamastran Valley proved particularly fertile, producing tobaccos that rivaled Cuba's legendary Vuelta Abajo region. Meanwhile, in the Dominican Republic's Cibao Valley, tobacco farmers introduced new curing techniques to enhance richness and complexity.

Genetic research also played a crucial role. Scientists focused on developing strains that were:
- More disease-resistant and capable of growing in diverse climates
- Able to replicate the depth and complexity of Cuban tobacco
- Sustainable for long-term production

This blending of traditional craftsmanship with scientific research marked a profound shift—one that would reshape the future of premium cigars.

The Art and Science of Fermentation: Unlocking Complexity

Curing and fermentation, once regarded as mystical processes, became fields of intense study. Cuban cigar makers had long relied on closely guarded fermentation techniques, but now manufacturers in exile sought ways to refine and even surpass traditional methods.

Climate-controlled fermentation rooms allowed for precise temperature and humidity regulation, ensuring that tobacco aged consistently. Some manufacturers experimented with extended fermentation periods, allowing flavors to develop even further. The result was a more consistent, refined product, one that could stand alongside Cuban cigars in complexity and richness.

Blending as a Craft: Beyond Cuban Replication

Before the embargo, Cuban cigars had been considered the pinnacle of luxury, their flavors defined by single-origin purity. But without Cuban leaf, manufacturers turned to multi-origin blending, treating cigar creation like a fine art akin to winemaking.

Brands like Padrón, Fuente, and Oliva pioneered the blending of tobaccos from multiple countries, crafting unique and complex flavor profiles. Some cigar makers meticulously combined leaves from Nicaragua, Honduras, and the Dominican Republic, treating each tobacco's strength, aroma, and texture as essential components of a carefully composed symphony.

This shift was more than necessity—it was a revolution. Cigar makers were no longer imitating Cuban cigars; they were creating something entirely new.

Packaging and Preservation: The Technology of Aging

Innovation extended beyond tobacco cultivation and blending. Humidity-control technology, advanced humidor designs, and sophisticated shipping methods ensured cigars could maintain their quality across international markets. Manufacturers also experimented with:

- Vacuum-sealed packaging to preserve freshness
- Controlled-aging humidors to replicate Cuba's natural aging process
- Climate-monitored storage facilities for precision aging

By the late 1980s, these innovations had transformed the cigar industry. What began as a forced adaptation had become a golden age of scientific advancement. The embargo, meant to cripple the industry, had inadvertently sparked a technological and artistic renaissance.

The scientific rebirth of tobacco had elevated the cigar industry beyond Cuba's borders, proving that true craftsmanship is not defined by location—but by a relentless pursuit of excellence.

WHAT DID THEY SMOKE?

Cigars as Symbols of Prestige, and Rebellion

While cigars remained linked to political power, as seen in earlier chapters, the embargo reshaped their cultural significance in America. No longer just symbols of leadership, they became markers of exclusivity, prestige, and quiet defiance. With Cuban cigars banned, their scarcity only heightened their allure. For the wealthy and well-connected, obtaining one was not just about quality—it was a statement. Smoking a Cuban cigar became an act of subtle rebellion, a way to display access to something forbidden.

Beyond politics, figures in business and entertainment embraced cigars as symbols of status and refinement. Hollywood icons, musicians, and executives adopted them as personal trademarks, reinforcing their image of success, indulgence, or nonconformity. More than ever, cigars became cultural artifacts—representing luxury, nostalgia, and, in some cases, a challenge to authority.

The Rebel Icons: Cigars in Hollywood and Music

Hollywood embraced cigars as a symbol of defiance and masculinity, using them to define characters who lived by their own rules. Marlon Brando's Don Vito Corleone in *The Godfather* wielded his Partagas cigar with deliberate authority, using slow, contemplative puffs to assert dominance without raising his voice. In real life, Brando himself saw cigars as a tool for presence and performance, often using them in interviews as an extension of his acting style.

Arnold Schwarzenegger helped revive cigar culture in the 1980s and 1990s, frequently appearing in films and magazine covers with a Davidoff or Punch cigar in hand. His love for cigars became part of his larger-than-life persona, reinforcing his image as a man of success, discipline, and indulgence. Similarly, actors like Sylvester Stallone, a Montecristo smoker, and Al Pacino, known for his preference for Cuban Cohibas, used cigars both on and off-screen to project an aura of power and rebellion.

Frank Sinatra and the Rat Pack turned cigars into an art form, blending sophistication with a rebellious streak. Their preference for brands like Bolivar and Montecristo added to their public personas—men of success, indulgence, and effortless cool. A night at the Sands in Las Vegas was never complete without a cigar in hand, a drink on the table, and a smooth jazz tune in the air.

African American jazz musicians also made cigars part of their personal brand. Miles Davis preferred Montecristo No. 2s, while Duke Ellington enjoyed Romeo y Julieta Cedros No. 1s. In an era of segregation and limited opportunities, cigars were a statement of dignity and artistic independence. They were more than a luxury—they were a symbol of cultural defiance, a way of occupying space in a world that often sought to marginalize them. Many of these musicians found cigars to be a form of relaxation and reflection, a break from the intensity of their performances and the challenges of their time.

The Corporate Ritual: Cigars as Social Currency

Beyond entertainment and politics, cigars played a powerful role in the world of business and high finance. In the boardrooms of IBM and the trading floors of Wall Street, premium cigars became part of the unwritten rules of power. Sharing a fine Cuban cigar before the embargo, or a Dominican-crafted alternative afterward, was a gesture of trust, negotiation, and status.

The Collectors: Cigars as Time Capsules of History

By the 1970s and 80s, Cuban cigars had become historical artifacts. As the embargo continued, pre-1962 cigars became sought-after collector's items, increasing in value each year. Wealthy enthusiasts preserved sealed boxes like rare art pieces, treating them as time capsules from a lost diplomatic era.

Private collectors often stored these rare cigars in climate-controlled vaults, ensuring their preservation for decades. Some pre-embargo cigars from the 1950s and 1960s have sold for tens of thousands of dollars, with collectors valuing them as both luxury items and historical relics. Auction houses like Sotheby's and Christie's have featured vintage cigars in their fine collectibles categories, further elevating their status in the world of high-end connoisseurship.

But while cigars retained their cultural and symbolic significance, the very foundation of the industry had been reshaped by political upheaval, forcing a global reinvention that would redefine the art of cigar-making.

Exile and Excellence: How the Cuban Embargo Reshaped the Cigar World

The story of post-embargo cigars is, at its core, a profoundly human narrative. It is a testament to adaptation, the creativity born from constraint, and the ability of cultural traditions to not just endure, but thrive under the most challenging circumstances. What once seemed like a devastating setback instead sparked a renaissance, as exiled cigar makers carried their expertise across the world, transforming the industry and elevating it to new heights.

This pattern of reinvention continues to define the modern cigar landscape. From the boutique boom of the 1990s to the surging demand in emerging luxury markets, cigars have proven their enduring appeal. Yet this transformation was more than economic—it was cultural. As new regions flourished and craftsmanship reached unprecedented levels, cigars reemerged as a statement of identity, refinement, and rebellion.

The very scarcity of Cuban cigars in the U.S. market only amplified their mystique, while non-Cuban brands fought to prove they could not only match but surpass the legendary Havana standards.

By the late 20th century, cigars had been fully reimagined. They were no longer just relics of a bygone era but a symbol of distinction in the modern world. They became cultural markers in entertainment, business, and politics, embraced by Hollywood icons, corporate leaders, and a new generation of collectors. With the rise of cigar lounges, magazines, and luxury branding, the industry found itself in the midst of an unexpected resurgence.

No longer confined to tradition, cigars were at the center of a revival that blended old-world craftsmanship with new-world accessibility. What followed was nothing short of a cigar renaissance—one driven by innovation, storytelling, and an evolving global audience eager to rediscover the art of the smoke. The 1990s would not just restore the prestige of cigars; it would redefine them for a new era.

"I had no idea whether or not
anyone was going to show up.
I had no way of knowing
when the idea started."

— MARVIN R. SHANKEN, founder and publisher of
Cigar Aficionado, recalling the first
Big Smoke event, May 1993

———

Shanken launched *Cigar Aficionado* in September 1992 into a market that had been declining for almost three decades. By every reasonable measure, the cigar business in 1992 was finished. Within five years, premium cigar imports would surge 66 percent in a single year and nearly quadruple from their 1992 baseline. The 1990s revival was not predicted. It happened anyway.

CHAPTER 5

The 1990s Cigar Revival

Post Cold War Prosperity | The 1991 collapse of the Soviet Union didn't just end the Cold War—it redrew the global balance of power, redefined economic systems, and reshaped cultural dynamics on an unprecedented scale. With the ideological battle between capitalism and communism over, the United States emerged as the undisputed global superpower. The 1990s ushered in a period of unprecedented economic expansion, technological revolution, and cultural transformation, creating an environment in which luxury markets— including cigars—could thrive once again.

Geopolitical Reconfiguration and the End of the Cold War

The dissolution of the Soviet Union was a geopolitical earthquake, giving rise to fifteen independent republics and transforming Eastern European nations into democracies with free-market economies. The Cold War's end not only eliminated the looming threat of nuclear confrontation but also redirected global priorities from military buildup to economic expansion and globalization.

For the United States, this was a moment of unparalleled global dominance. With no military rival to counter its influence, American culture, business, and finance expanded rapidly across the world. The 1990s became an era defined by free-market policies, deregulation, and global trade, fueling an economic boom that elevated luxury industries—including premium cigars—to new heights.

Economic Expansion and the "Long Boom"

The U.S. economy flourished throughout the 1990s, fueled by low unemployment, rising incomes, and technological advancements. Key economic indicators reflect the strength of this "Long Boom":

- The Dow Jones Industrial Average skyrocketed from 2,700 in 1991 to over 11,000 by 1999, reflecting booming investor confidence.
- Unemployment dropped to just 4 percent by 2000, the lowest in decades.
- The federal budget moved from deficit to surplus for the first time in over 30 years.
- The emerging tech sector revolutionized industries, creating the "dot-com economy."

This economic boom fueled consumer demand for luxury goods, including premium cigars. As corporate executives, Wall Street financiers, and Hollywood elites embraced a culture of indulgence, cigars became a status symbol of power and success.

The Technological Revolution and Global Connectivity

The 1990s witnessed a technological transformation that reshaped business, communication, and social life. The personal computer became a household staple, and the internet—once a niche government tool—exploded into mainstream use. By the end of the decade, more than half of American households were online, and companies like Microsoft, Apple, Amazon, and Google were growing into global powerhouses.

This new digital age helped drive globalization, enabling luxury goods, media, and cultural trends to reach consumers worldwide. For the cigar industry, this meant greater visibility, easier access to information, and a newfound interest in traditional craftsmanship—setting the stage for the Cigar Boom of the 1990s.

Cultural Shifts and the Rise of Consumer Luxury

Economic prosperity and technological advancements in the 1990s fueled major cultural shifts. A new class of young, tech-savvy entrepreneurs joined the traditional corporate elite, embracing symbols of old-world luxury—fine cigars, aged whiskey, and tailored suits—as markers of success.

Consumer culture flourished, driving demand for high-end goods. Department stores, boutique brands, and luxury publications thrived, catering to an audience eager for indulgence. *Cigar Aficionado* magazine, launched in 1992, captured this moment perfectly, elevating cigars from a declining tradition to a revitalized status symbol.

Globalization and the Reshaping of Trade

With the Cold War over, global trade barriers loosened, and American businesses expanded aggressively into new markets. The establishment of the World Trade Organization (1995) further accelerated international commerce, while corporate consolidation and financial deregulation helped create a powerful, consumer-driven global economy.

For the cigar industry, this new era of globalization had two major effects:
1. Luxury markets expanded, creating a global appetite for premium cigars, particularly in the U.S. and Europe.
2. Cuban cigars, still banned in the U.S. due to the embargo, gained a mythical status, increasing demand on the black market and fueling the rise of Nicaraguan, Dominican, and Honduran cigars as top-tier alternatives.

Challenges and Contradictions

Despite the overwhelming prosperity, the 1990s were not without their economic and social contradictions:
• Income inequality widened, as wealth concentrated among investors and corporate executives, while rural and industrial communities faced stagnation.

- The dot-com bubble, which fueled much of the decade's economic optimism, was already showing signs of overinflated growth—setting the stage for its dramatic collapse in 2000.
- Financial deregulation, which encouraged aggressive speculation, would later contribute to the financial crises of the early 2000s and 2008.

Nevertheless, the optimism and affluence of the 1990s created a fertile ground for cultural indulgence, which included the resurgence of cigar smoking as a marker of success and sophistication.

In summary, the 1990s was a decade of transformation and reinvention, defined by post-Cold War optimism, economic expansion, and technological revolution. As global capitalism flourished, consumer luxury markets thrived, and cigars—long associated with power and status—became the ultimate indulgence of the era.

With money flowing, stock markets soaring, and cultural attitudes shifting toward leisure and celebration, the cigar industry was primed for an extraordinary comeback. This chapter explores how the 'cigar boom of the 1990s' brought cigars back into the mainstream, fueled by a new generation of consumers, celebrity culture, and the growing influence of cigar media.

The Unexpected Comeback

By the late 1980s, premium cigars had all but disappeared from mainstream American smoking culture, seemingly destined for obsolescence. The industry had suffered decades of decline due to the Cuban Embargo, changing smoking habits, and increasing government regulations. Cigarette consumption had skyrocketed, and cigars—once a staple of affluence and influence—were now seen as a fading relic of the past. Sales plummeted, cigar lounges shuttered, and even historic brands struggled to remain relevant.

Then, in a remarkable cultural shift, cigars made an unexpected and dramatic return in the 1990s. Almost overnight, they were back in the spotlight, embraced by high-powered executives, Hollywood stars, professional athletes, and politicians. A new wave of boutique cigar brands reinvigorated the industry, while media coverage—particularly the launch of *Cigar Aficionado* magazine—helped fuel the craze.

The cigar boom of the 1990s was more than just a market resurgence—it was the rebirth of an entire cultural movement. This chapter explores the forces that ignited this revival, the role of media and celebrity culture, the rise of boutique brands, and the lasting impact of this golden age of cigar smoking.

Hollywood, Celebrity Culture, and the Resurgence of Cigars

The cigar's resurgence wasn't orchestrated by marketing campaigns—it was driven by something far more powerful: the influence of cultural icons. Hollywood stars, sports legends, and public figures became the unexpected ambassadors of tobacco's reinvention. What had once been a diminishing habit of previous generations was suddenly redefined as a statement of confidence, sophistication, and success.

Hollywood was instrumental in reshaping this image. Celebrities weren't just smoking cigars; they were redefining them as symbols of personal power and achievement. No one embodied this transformation more than Arnold Schwarzenegger. The action star wasn't just an aficionado—he was a cigar evangelist, lobbying for cigar-friendly policies in California and appearing in magazine spreads that made cigar smoking an aspirational act.

In sports, Michael Jordan elevated the cigar into something more than just a luxury item—it became a trophy of success. At the peak of his dominance, Jordan's post-championship ritual of smoking Cuban cigars in the locker room became an enduring image of triumph. For a generation of sports fans, his cigar was less about tobacco and more about achievement, celebration, and personal power.

Meanwhile, Hollywood's storytelling reinforced the cultural cachet of cigars. Films like *The Godfather* had long cemented cigars as symbols of power and criminal sophistication, and *Casino* added a new layer in 1995.

The Sopranos, premiering in 1999, took it even further—embedding cigars into the visual language of masculinity, status, and cultural identity. Every puff became a performance of power, wealth, and influence.

Actors like Sylvester Stallone, Bruce Willis, and Jack Nicholson didn't just smoke cigars—they made them an extension of their personal style. Even Madonna challenged gender norms by incorporating cigars into her public image, transforming them into a statement of rebellious sophistication.

By the mid-1990s, cigars had undergone a remarkable transformation. No longer a forgotten habit of past generations, they had been redefined as a cultural artifact—a symbol of reinvention, success, and defiance in an era of economic expansion and evolving social norms.

The Launch of Cigar Aficionado: Architecting a Cultural Renaissance

If celebrities provided the visual language of the cigar revival, Marvin Shanken provided its literary architecture. Where Hollywood created the image, Shanken crafted the narrative. In 1992, he launched *Cigar Aficionado* and engineered a cultural renaissance that transformed cigars from a declining consumer product into a sophisticated lifestyle choice.

The magazine was a masterpiece of cultural engineering. Where traditional tobacco publications had focused on technical details and consumption, *Cigar Aficionado* crafted a comprehensive mythology around cigars. Each issue was less a product guide and more a manifesto of aspiration—positioning cigars as artifacts of success, masculinity, and refined taste.

Visually, the magazine was revolutionary. Meticulously art-directed spreads juxtaposed cigars with symbols of luxury—gleaming sports cars, Swiss watches, private jets—creating a visual language that transcended tobacco consumption. Celebrities weren't just photographed with cigars; they were transformed into cultural ambassadors of a new cigar lifestyle, reinforcing the brand's aspirational messaging.

Arnold Schwarzenegger on the cover of Cigar Aficionado (1996). The action star's public embrace of cigars during the 1990s helped solidify their status as symbols of power, success, and sophistication. This iconic cover captures the connection between celebrity culture and the cigar renaissance, reflecting how Hollywood figures became key ambassadors for premium cigars in the era of economic boom and cultural reinvention.

The editorial strategy was equally sophisticated. Detailed ratings, brand histories, and industry insights provided a veneer of expertise that attracted both seasoned smokers and curious newcomers. By demystifying cigar culture while simultaneously making it more exclusive, Shanken created a powerful marketing ecosystem that engaged consumers at every level.

Beyond a publication, *Cigar Aficionado* became a cultural movement. It generated entire economic ecosystems—spawning specialty shops, lounges, and a renewed interest in premium tobacco production. Brands that might have disappeared found new life through the magazine's carefully curated narratives of craftsmanship and tradition, securing cigars as an enduring symbol of affluence and sophistication.

The Boutique Cigar Renaissance: Crafting a New Tobacco Mythology

While *Cigar Aficionado* created the cultural blueprint, a new generation of tobacco artisans would provide its most compelling content. These weren't merely manufacturers, but cultural alchemists transforming raw tobacco into narratives of heritage and innovation.

This renaissance was defined by a radical philosophy: quality was not just a marketing term, but a comprehensive approach to tobacco production. Brands like Padron, Fuente, and Drew Estate didn't just make cigars; they created complex narratives of cultural heritage, agricultural innovation, and personal craftsmanship.

Padron's 1964 Anniversary Series represented this ethos perfectly. Founded by Cuban exile José Orlando Padrón, the brand embodied resilience and precision. Each cigar was a testament to displacement and reinvention—tobacco grown in Nicaraguan soil, rolled by hands that carried generations of Cuban expertise. The limited production and meticulous aging process transformed each cigar into more than a product; it became a cultural artifact.

Fuente Fuente Opus X achieved something revolutionary. By creating the first successful all-Dominican premium cigar, the Fuente family challenged the long-standing belief that exceptional tobacco could only come from Cuba. Their success was a powerful statement about the global democratization of cigar production post-embargo.

Drew Estate represented the most radical reimagining of cigar culture. Founded in 1996, the brand didn't just produce cigars—they deconstructed and reconstructed the entire concept of tobacco consumption. Their flavored and experimental blends appealed to a younger, more diverse audience, expanding the traditional boundaries of cigar appreciation.

Brands like Rocky Patel, La Flor Dominicana, and Ashton further solidified this new paradigm. They weren't just selling cigars; they were selling experiences, crafting luxury narratives that elevated tobacco from a simple consumer product to a sophisticated lifestyle choice.

The boutique movement was ultimately a declaration that small-scale craftsmanship could triumph over industrial standardization. Each carefully rolled cigar became a small rebellion against mass production, a handcrafted testament to human skill and tradition.

The Global Tobacco Ecosystem: A Renaissance Without Borders

The boutique revolution was never meant to be contained within national borders. What began as a local renaissance would quickly transform into a global tobacco dialogue, reshaping international trade and cultural exchange. The 1990s cigar boom was more than an American phenomenon. It redefined tobacco production worldwide. As the United States rediscovered its passion for premium cigars, a complex international network of tobacco producers, distributors, and enthusiasts emerged, creating an unprecedented global tobacco ecosystem.

Nicaragua, the Dominican Republic, and Honduras became the primary beneficiaries of this cultural shift. These nations were no longer mere alternatives to Cuban tobacco—they became innovators, transforming their agricultural and manufacturing approaches to meet the surging global demand. In Nicaragua's Estelí region, volcanic soils became a laboratory of tobacco innovation. Farmers who had learned traditional techniques from Cuban exiles now developed distinctive growing methods that would come to define a new era of cigar production.

By the 1990s, the global cigar industry had fully adapted to the absence of Cuban imports in the U.S. market, creating a sophisticated international trade network. Tobacco brokers, once reliant on Cuban suppliers, had long since developed deep connections across the Dominican Republic, Nicaragua, and Honduras. Shipping routes expanded, distribution channels grew more complex, and new brands emerged to meet surging demand. The cigar boom of the decade transformed what had once been a Cuban-dominated trade into a dynamic, multi-national industry, with each region carving out its own reputation for excellence.

European markets played a crucial role in this transformation. While the United States had been cut off from Cuban cigars, European countries maintained robust trade relationships. Cities like London, Paris, and Madrid became global hubs of cigar culture, with high-end tobacconists and exclusive smoking clubs that maintained the traditional European approach to cigar appreciation.

The technological exchange became equally significant. Agricultural scientists from different countries began collaborating, sharing knowledge about soil composition, curing techniques, and tobacco hybridization. What had been closely guarded national secrets became an international dialogue of tobacco expertise. Nicaraguan farmers learned from Dominican growing techniques, while Honduran manufacturers adopted innovative Cuban-inspired rolling methods.

The impact of the 1990s cigar boom extended well into the 21st century, reshaping the industry's cultural and commercial landscape. International tobacco exhibitions and trade shows became essential networking platforms, reflecting the globalization of premium cigars. The ProCigar Festival, first held in 2008 in the Dominican Republic, and Nicaragua's Puro Sabor Festival, launched in 2012, transformed these gatherings from industry meetings into global celebrations of craftsmanship. These festivals continue to bring together tobacco experts, farmers, manufacturers, and enthusiasts for factory tours, tastings, and discussions on blending techniques—highlighting national traditions while fostering innovation and collaboration across borders.

This global ecosystem challenged traditional notions of tobacco production. The myth of Cuban tobacco supremacy was gradually replaced by a more nuanced understanding of terroir, craftsmanship, and innovation. Cigars were no longer defined by their country of origin, but by the skill of their makers, the quality of their tobacco, and the complexity of their blends.

By the late 1990s, the global tobacco landscape had been completely reimagined. Cigars had become a truly global product, a complex cultural artifact that transcended national boundaries. The embargo that was meant to isolate Cuba had instead created a vibrant, interconnected international tobacco culture.

The Growth of Cigar Lounges: Redefining Social Capital

Beyond magazines and brands, the cigar renaissance demanded physical spaces of ritual and connection. These weren't just smoking rooms, but carefully choreographed stages where power, masculinity, and social capital would be performed and negotiated.

Establishments like the Grand Havana Room in New York and Beverly Hills represented a new architectural language of exclusivity. These were not simply smoking spaces, but carefully designed social laboratories. Meticulously crafted interiors, with rich mahogany paneling, leather armchairs, and carefully curated lighting, created environments that were simultaneously nostalgic and forward-looking. They evoked the gentlemen's clubs of the early 20th century while speaking to a new generation of professional and cultural elites.

The social dynamics of these lounges were complex and multilayered. Business deals were negotiated not in sterile conference rooms, but in environments where the slow ritual of cigar smoking created a unique conversational space. The act of cutting, lighting, and slowly consuming a premium cigar became a form of social choreography—a performance of masculinity, sophistication, and professional success.

Events like *Cigar Aficionado*'s "Big Smoke" further transformed cigar consumption into a collective cultural experience[8]. These gatherings were more than trade shows; they were social rituals that allowed enthusiasts to perform their identity, network, and participate in a shared cultural moment. Industry insiders, celebrities, and passionate amateurs mingled, creating a democratic yet exclusive social ecosystem.

Venues like Casa de Montecristo and Club Macanudo did more than sell cigars—they sold an experience of belonging. The pairing of premium cigars with aged whiskeys and fine dining created a multisensory cultural performance. Each lounge became a stage where personal and professional identities could be carefully crafted and displayed.

By the late 1990s, these lounges had become more than smoking venues. They were complex social technologies—spaces where class, masculinity, professional aspiration, and cultural capital were continuously negotiated and performed.

WHAT DID THEY SMOKE?

The Celebrities and Cigars of the 1990s Boom

Behind every cultural transformation are individual stories. The celebrities of the 1990s didn't just smoke cigars—they turned them into statements of personal identity. Each carefully chosen brand became a symbol of status, power, and success, reinforcing the broader cultural shift that made cigars an essential accessory of affluence.

Arnold Schwarzenegger epitomized the era's cigar culture. Known for his preference for Cuban Montecristos before the embargo, he transitioned to Nicaraguan Padróns during the boom years. His public cigar smoking wasn't just a habit—it was a performance of masculinity and success, often

---

[8] *Cigar Aficionado*'s Big Smoke debuted on May 19, 1993, in New York City, evolving into a premier cigar event that blended luxury, networking, and culture. Its success led to expansion, with Las Vegas hosting its first Big Smoke in 1995. These gatherings transformed cigar consumption into a collective experience, uniting industry insiders, celebrities, and enthusiasts in a dynamic social ecosystem. Big Smoke events continue today, remaining a premier gathering for cigar enthusiasts.

photographed with large ring gauge cigars that matched his outsized Hollywood persona.

Michael Jordan transformed the cigar from a post-game indulgence into a symbol of athletic triumph. His favorite was the Cuban Partagás Lusitania — a double corona he smoked openly, embargo or not, as Cigar Aficionado itself documented in interviews with him. Each championship cigar became a cultural moment, capturing the intersection of sports, achievement, and cigar culture.

Hollywood's elite became walking advertisements for premium cigars. Jack Nicholson favored large ring gauge Fuente Fuente Opus X, while Bruce Willis was often seen with Rocky Patel cigars. These weren't just smoking choices—they were carefully curated extensions of personal brand and sophistication, reinforcing the cultural cachet of cigars.

Even musicians joined the trend. Rapper and actor Ice Cube was frequently photographed with Drew Estate's flavored cigars, representing the brand's appeal to younger, more diverse audiences. Madonna's cigar smoking, however, was as much about image as indulgence. While no single brand is definitively linked to her, she often chose bold, statement-making cigars that complemented her rebellious persona.

On *The Late Show with David Letterman* in 1994, Madonna brazenly smoked a cigar on air, turning it into a provocative act that challenged gender norms. Whether calculated or not, the image stuck and the cigar became part of her performance of defiance and artistic identity, a visual symbol of power that women were not supposed to claim.

Meanwhile, behind the scenes, cigar makers became as celebrated as the celebrities who smoked their products. Carlos Fuente Jr. of Arturo Fuente and José Orlando Padrón were themselves becoming cultural icons, their brands representing more than just tobacco—they embodied stories of immigrant success, craftsmanship, and reinvention.

The most telling detail wasn't just what they smoked, but how they smoked. Cigars were no longer just a luxury product—they became a performance of masculinity, success, rebellion, and cultural sophistication. Each puff was a statement, each brand a carefully chosen narrative of personal identity, cementing cigars as an enduring symbol of power in the 1990s.

Conclusion: A Boom That Transformed an Industry

The cigar renaissance of the 1990s was more than a market trend—it was a profound cultural metamorphosis. What had begun as a niche revival had fundamentally reshaped the landscape of tobacco consumption, creating a new paradigm of craftsmanship, luxury, and cultural identity. By the late 1990s, the industry faced the inevitable challenges of rapid growth. Overproduction and market saturation threatened to undermine the very renaissance that had breathed new life into cigar culture. Yet, the cultural shift unleashed during this period proved far more enduring than any economic fluctuation.

The boom had accomplished something remarkable. Premium cigars evolved from relics of past generations into dynamic cultural artifacts. Boutique cigar makers had established a new gold standard of craftsmanship, transforming tobacco production from an industrial process to an artisanal art form. Brands like Padron, Fuente, and Drew Estate had done more than create cigars—they had written a new narrative of cultural heritage and innovation.

More profoundly, the 1990s had democratized the premium cigar culture. What was once an exclusive domain of wealthy executives and Hollywood elites had become a more inclusive space. Younger, more diverse audiences found themselves drawn to the ritual, complexity, and social significance of premium cigars.

The industry that had nearly collapsed in the 1980s was now a vibrant, innovative ecosystem. Cigar lounges, magazines, and international events had created a global community united by a shared appreciation for craftsmanship and tradition. The boundaries between producer and consumer had blurred, creating a more engaged, passionate tobacco culture.

As the millennium turned, cigars were no longer just a relic of the past—they were entering a new era of artistry, experimentation, and boutique craftsmanship.

A torcedora at her chaveta board. The boutique movement returned cigar-making to hands like these.

CHAPTER 6

The Boutique Cigar Renaissance

The Rise of Craftmanship | The modern world is built on mass production. For over a century, industrialization and globalization prioritized efficiency, standardization, and scale, making consumer goods more affordable and accessible. But in this pursuit of uniformity, something fundamental was lost—the personal connection between maker and product that had defined human production for millennia.

By the late 20th and early 21st centuries, a cultural shift was underway. Consumers, fatigued by identical products churned out by faceless corporations, began seeking authenticity, artistry, and individuality. From fashion to food, brewing to cigars, a new wave of craftsmanship emerged, rejecting industrial uniformity in favor of small-batch production, quality over quantity, and storytelling over mass appeal.

This craftsmanship renaissance was fundamentally a philosophical and economic movement, redefining value and creativity in an age of automation.

The Backlash Against Mass Production

For most of the 20th century, the world embraced the model of mass manufacturing. Henry Ford's assembly line revolution and the rise of global supply chains made goods cheaper and more accessible than ever before.

Every industry—from automobiles to food, clothing to cigars—became focused on producing at scale, driving down costs, and maximizing efficiency.

But by the late 20th century, the cracks in this model became apparent. Globalization blurred cultural uniqueness, with products made thousands of miles away from where they were consumed. Corporations prioritized profit over craftsmanship, creating goods that were more affordable yet inferior in quality. The consumer experience became increasingly impersonal, detached, and commodified.

In response, a growing movement sought to reclaim craftsmanship, restoring a sense of individuality and artistry to everyday goods.

The Cultural Shift Toward Authenticity

The rise of craftsmanship wasn't just about nostalgia—it was a reaction to the economic and technological shifts of the modern world. Several forces drove this movement:

1. Economic Disillusionment – The 2008 financial crisis shattered public trust in large corporations, revealing the fragility of global markets. As faith in massive institutions declined, consumers gravitated toward smaller, more transparent businesses that valued craftsmanship over cost-cutting.

2. The Technological Paradox – The same digital revolution that made industrial production more efficient also allowed small-scale artisans to reach global audiences. Platforms like Etsy, Instagram, and Kickstarter enabled independent makers to sell handcrafted goods worldwide, challenging the dominance of corporate retail.

3. Environmental and Ethical Consciousness – As awareness of sustainability and fair labor practices grew, consumers began rejecting mass-produced, disposable goods in favor of ethically sourced, durable alternatives. The philosophy of "buy less, but buy better" became central to the craft movement.

4. The Desire for Individuality – In a world of identical, mass-produced items, craftsmanship became a form of self-expression. Whether it was custom suits, hand-crafted furniture, small-batch bourbon, or boutique

cigars, consumers sought products with a story—unique, high-quality, and deeply personal.

The Craft Movement Across Industries

This craftsmanship renaissance reshaped multiple sectors:

- Craft Beer & Spirits – The number of craft breweries exploded from nearly zero in 1980 to over 8,000 by 2019, paralleled by a similar rise in small-batch bourbon and whiskey distilleries. Bourbon, in particular, became a luxury item with deep American roots, much like cigars. Premium brands like Buffalo Trace, Pappy Van Winkle, and Angel's Envy turned bourbon into an art form, with aging, barrel selection, and blending techniques rivaling those of fine wine.
- Specialty Coffee & Artisanal Food – The rise of single-origin coffee, small-batch chocolate, and farm-to-table dining emphasized authenticity and craftsmanship. Consumers were willing to pay more for products that told a story of origin, skill, and personal connection.
- Bespoke Fashion – The resurgence of custom tailoring, handcrafted leather goods, and small-batch clothing brands reflected a rejection of fast fashion in favor of quality and individuality.
- Maker Culture & Small-Batch Tech – Platforms like Kickstarter and 3D printing communities empowered inventors and small-scale manufacturers to bring unique, highly crafted products to market.

At its core, the craft movement sought to reestablish human skill and artistry in production, profoundly impacting the cigar industry.

The Boutique Cigar Renaissance

Nowhere was this craftsmanship revival more evident than in the boutique cigar movement. While mass-produced cigars still dominated the market, a new generation of tobacco artisans emerged, reshaping industry expectations. These boutique manufacturers rejected uniformity in favor of small-scale, meticulous production, crafting cigars that prioritized innovation, heritage, and superior quality over mass appeal.

Rather than relying on traditional formulas, boutique brands explored new growing regions, fermentation techniques, and aging methods, developing blends with distinctive character. Some cigars were aged for years before release, similar to fine bourbons and premium whiskeys, yielding richer, more complex flavors. Expert artisans played a central role, using handcrafted rolling techniques to preserve time-honored traditions that industrialization had once threatened.

Beyond the product itself, boutique manufacturers redefined the experience of cigar appreciation. Limited production runs transformed select cigars into coveted collector's items, while brand storytelling deepened the connection between the smoker and the cigar's origins. Every aspect of production—from the tobacco fields to the hands of the master roller—became part of a larger narrative celebrating artistry and tradition.

Unlike large-scale manufacturers focused on efficiency and consistency, boutique cigar makers sought to reinvigorate the culture of craftsmanship. Their cigars weren't just products; they were expressions of skill and creativity, designed to appeal to aficionados who valued the artistry behind every draw.

This movement, beyond bringing innovation to cigar making, also shifted the industry's priorities from sheer output to quality, complexity, and authenticity. The boutique cigar renaissance wasn't a passing trend; it was a return to craftsmanship in its purest form, proving that cigars could be more than a luxury item—they could be a deeply personal and artistic pursuit.

The Meaning of Craftsmanship

Beyond business and marketing, the craft movement was rooted in deeper ideas about human creativity, labor, and meaning. In his book *The Craftsman*, Richard Sennett argues that craftsmanship is a fundamental human impulse—the desire to create something well for its own sake. This idea, that work can be both functional and fulfilling, was at the heart of the boutique cigar renaissance.

In a world that increasingly prioritized speed, automation, and mass production, craftsmanship stood as a countercultural force, reminding people that the best things take time, skill, and passion to create.

Beyond a Trend

The craftsmanship renaissance wasn't just about cigars, beer, or fashion—it was a cultural shift in how people valued quality, heritage, and artistry. It represented a rejection of mass consumerism, a rediscovery of individuality, and a reimagining of production in the modern world.

For the cigar industry, this was a reinvention. What had once been an industry of big factories and mass-market blends was now a world of handcrafted excellence, boutique artistry, and deeply personal craftsmanship.

Far from being a nostalgic retreat, this movement was forward-looking—a vision of an economy where tradition and innovation coexist, where creativity thrives, and where craftsmanship remains not just relevant, but essential.

A New Golden Age for Cigar Craftsmanship

By the turn of the 21st century, the cigar industry stood at a crossroads. The 1990s boom, fueled by celebrity culture, *Cigar Aficionado*, and a resurgence of luxury branding, had propelled cigars back into the mainstream. But as with any trend, the excitement eventually cooled. Sales dipped from their late-90s peak, large corporations tightened their grip on distribution, and some cigar companies failed to survive the post-boom correction. Many expected the industry to fade once again into the background, a relic of a past era.

Instead, something remarkable happened. The dawn of the 21st century marked a profound transformation in cigar production—a moment when craftsmanship transcended industrial efficiency. The early 2000s ushered in a boutique cigar renaissance, where small, independent brands challenged industry giants by prioritizing innovation and artistry. This movement, led by a new generation of blenders and growers, revitalized cigars as more than just a luxury product—they became an artisanal pursuit, where terroir, blending techniques, and aging processes were reimagined.

In the early 21st century, several vintage American cigar brands experienced a remarkable resurrection, bridging nostalgic craftsmanship with modern production techniques. A few examples include Cremo Cigars, originally established in 1896 as a 5¢ cigar brand, which now produces premium cigars while paying homage to its historical roots. 7-20-4, a revived old-school brand, now combines premium tobaccos from multiple countries, creating a contemporary interpretation of its historical roots. Similarly, Brick House, originally launched in 1937 by J.C. Newman, was relaunched by the founder's grandsons using Nicaraguan tobaccos, preserving the brand's legacy while appealing to modern cigar enthusiasts.

These revivals represent more than mere commercial strategies—they are passionate efforts to honor and reinvent America's rich cigar-making heritage. Where mass-market manufacturing had once dominated, a new generation of artisan cigar makers emerged, treating tobacco not as a commodity, but as a complex cultural artifact.

This boutique renaissance was more than a marketing strategy; it was a philosophical revolution. These new manufacturers rejected the standardization that had characterized cigar production for decades. Instead, they approached tobacco with the same reverence a vintner might approach wine or a master chef might approach rare ingredients. Traditional manufacturers had focused on consistency and volume; these new artisans prioritized complexity, rarity, and individual expression.

It was no longer enough to simply roll cigars; the best brands told a story, honored tradition, and pushed the boundaries of what a cigar could be. They sourced tobaccos from specific microclimates, experimenting with fermentation techniques that had been forgotten or ignored by larger manufacturers. Some aged their tobaccos for years, treating each leaf as a living, evolving entity.

The remainder of this chapter explores how the boutique revolution transformed cigar culture in the 21st century, how American-grown tobacco has seen an unexpected revival, and how the digital age has reshaped the way cigars are marketed, discussed, appreciated, and enjoyed.

Key Innovators of the Boutique Movement

Several boutique cigar brands emerged as trailblazers, redefining craftsmanship and elevating cigars into a more refined, small-batch experience. These brands weren't just manufacturers; they were industry disruptors, pushing the boundaries of blending, aging, and production techniques.

Drew Estate became one of the most revolutionary names of this new era. Founded by Jonathan Drew, the company challenged industry norms with its unconventional approach. The *Acid* line introduced infused cigars that broadened the appeal of premium tobacco, while *Liga Privada* showcased meticulously blended, full-bodied Nicaraguan tobaccos that redefined depth and complexity.

Tatuaje, created by Pete Johnson in collaboration with Cuban master blender Don José "Pepín" García, bridged the gap between Cuban tradition and boutique experimentation. Johnson's blends revived old-world rolling techniques while utilizing high-quality Nicaraguan tobacco, crafting cigars that delivered rich, complex flavors reminiscent of pre-embargo Cubans.

Illusione and Warped Cigars took the boutique concept even further. Illusione, founded by Dion Giolito, built a cult following with cigars that emphasized purity of tobacco, sourcing exclusively from Aganorsa's famed Nicaraguan fields. Each blend was carefully calibrated for balance, complexity, and a signature elegance. Warped Cigars, led by Kyle Gellis, revived a vintage Cuban aesthetic, combining old-school craftsmanship with a modern sensibility, appealing to enthusiasts who valued refinement over power.

What set these brands apart wasn't just their size, but their commitment to quality over quantity, innovation over mass production. Instead of competing with legacy brands on volume, they focused on pushing the limits of flavor, texture, and aging techniques.

By the second decade of the 21st century, these innovators had fundamentally reshaped cigar culture. What had once been a niche approach had become a dominant paradigm, proving that small-batch artistry could rival, and in some cases surpass, the output of century-old industry giants.

The Insightful Parallel Revival of Bourbon and Cigars

As boutique cigars redefined tobacco craftsmanship, a similar revival was reshaping bourbon. Once overshadowed by Scotch whisky and mass-market spirits, bourbon experienced a renaissance in the early 2000s as distillers embraced small-batch production, unique barrel aging, and historical recipes. Like premium cigars, bourbon evolved beyond a mere product—it became a sensory experience, a cultural statement, and a tribute to American heritage.

Limited-edition releases, single-barrel bourbons, and experimental aging techniques fueled this resurgence, mirroring the boutique cigar industry's focus on craftsmanship, terroir-driven blends, and meticulous aging. Both industries thrived on exclusivity, where rarity and tradition elevated the experience.

Pairing fine bourbon with boutique cigars became a ritual of appreciation. Enthusiasts pursued depth, complexity, and craftsmanship in both, much like a sommelier pairing wine with cuisine. The connection between cigars and bourbon extended beyond taste; it was rooted in shared principles of heritage, regional character, and the mastery of blending and aging.

This renewed reverence for terroir, time-honored techniques, and locally sourced ingredients was part of a broader revival of American craftsmanship, rekindling appreciation for one of the oldest traditions in premium tobacco: cigars crafted exclusively with American-grown tobacco.

Rediscovering Domestic Terroir

The story of cigars made with American-grown tobacco runs deeper than recent trends suggest. While international tobacco has dominated premium cigar manufacturing for much of the past century, several American manufacturers—though not boutique—have upheld the tradition of all-American tobacco cigars. The Finck Cigar Company, established in San Antonio in the 1880s, remains one of America's longest-running cigar makers, producing both handmade and machine-made cigars throughout its history. Similarly, Avanti Cigar Company, founded in 1901, has specialized in machine-made, dry-cured cigars crafted from Kentucky and Tennessee fire-cured tobacco, preserving a distinct American tradition.

What we are witnessing today isn't so much a revolution as it is a renaissance—a renewed appreciation for American tobacco's potential in premium cigars. This revival represents a sophisticated reclamation of agricultural heritage, a deliberate exploration of how American terroir can produce world-class tobacco. In Miami's Little Havana and other cigar-making centers, boutique manufacturers began to view domestic tobacco not as a compromise, but as a unique expression of regional character.

Connecticut emerged as a particularly compelling narrative. The state's tobacco-growing regions, with their rich alluvial soils and precise microclimate, had long been known to produce exceptional wrapper leaves. Connecticut Broadleaf and Connecticut Shade tobaccos, which had been staples in cigar production for generations, have found new appreciation among craft cigar makers seeking complexity and nuance.

Pennsylvania Broadleaf told an equally compelling story. Farmers in the Keystone State had maintained tobacco-growing traditions passed down through generations. Now, boutique blenders have discovered the leaf's bold, earthy profile—a distinctive flavor that speaks to the region's agricultural heritage. Brands have begun featuring Pennsylvania Broadleaf not as a secondary ingredient, but as a prized component in premium blends.

Perhaps most revolutionary has been Kentucky's contribution. The state's fire-cured tobacco tradition, long associated with pipe and chewing tobacco, has found an unexpected home in premium cigars. The introduction of fire-cured tobacco into premium cigar blends introduced a radical new flavor profile—smoky, almost campfire-like—that challenged traditional notions of cigar taste.

Among the manufacturers exploring all-American tobacco blends, G.R. Tabacaleras Co. Cigar Factory of Little Havana added their contribution in 2013 with the George Rico Miami "American Puro," crafted from Pennsylvania, Connecticut, and Kentucky tobaccos. This release joined a small number of Miami-based manufacturers experimenting with domestic tobacco blends.

Lancaster County, Pennsylvania (1938). Tobacco hanging in the barn on the Enos Royer farm.

The movement has continued to gain momentum with other manufacturers joining the exploration of domestic tobacco. The J.C. Newman Cigar Company's The American in 2019 and Ultimo Cigars' American Puro 2024 have further expanded the possibilities of domestic tobacco blends, each offering their own interpretation of what an American puro[9] can be.

---

[9] "American Puro" is a relatively new term in the industry. Traditionally, "puro" refers to a cigar made entirely from tobacco grown in a single country, such as a Cuban or Nicaraguan puro. While not yet a widely accepted classification, some brands have begun using the term to describe cigars made exclusively from U.S.-grown tobacco.

The Antebellum brand, launched in 2025, represents the next chapter in American cigar craftsmanship. As a true American Puro, it pays homage to a tradition dating back to the early 1800s, blending heritage with modern artisanal techniques. Crafted from carefully aged domestic tobaccos, each hand-rolled cigar delivers a bold yet refined smoking experience, bridging the past and present of American tobacco culture.[10]

This resurgence represents more than a trend. It is a profound recalibration of how we understand tobacco production. Domestic growers are no longer seen as secondary players, but as crucial innovators in a global craft. Each leaf tells a story of soil, climate, and human expertise—a narrative as complex and nuanced as the cigars themselves.

The cigar made entirely with American-grown tobacco movement demonstrates that true craftsmanship knows no borders. It is a testament to the ongoing reinvention of tradition, a celebration of local expertise, and a bold reimagining of what American tobacco can represent.

The Growth of Luxury Cigar Lounges & Private Clubs: Crafting a New Social Ecosystem

The evolution of cigar culture in the early 21st century has transcended mere consumption—it has become a sophisticated social performance. Luxury cigar lounges are no longer just smoking spaces; they are carefully curated cultural hubs that redefine the social rituals surrounding tobacco. These lounges represent a complex intersection of exclusivity, craftsmanship, and networking. They are architectural expressions of a new cigar philosophy—spaces where smoking is a carefully choreographed experience of sensory and social engagement.

The Grand Havana Room, with its exclusive locations in New York and Beverly Hills, epitomizes this new paradigm. More than a smoking venue, it is a social laboratory where Hollywood elites, Wall Street executives, and cultural influencers converge. The club's invitation-only model has transformed cigar smoking from a personal habit into a marker of social capital.

---

[10] Disclosure: The author is a creator of the Antebellum brand and founder of The American Cigar Co. He has worked to evaluate Antebellum on the same terms as the other brands discussed in this chapter.

Casa de Montecristo has pioneered a different approach, creating spaces that bridge traditional cigar culture with contemporary design. Their lounges in Chicago, South Florida, and New York blend old-world charm with modern aesthetics, appealing to a new generation of cigar enthusiasts who value both heritage and innovation.

Club Macanudo in New York City takes the concept even further. Here, cigar smoking is integrated into a comprehensive sensory experience. Fine dining, curated whiskey selections, and meticulously designed interiors elevate the act of smoking into a holistic cultural ritual. Each visit becomes a performance of sophistication, a carefully staged encounter with craftsmanship and tradition.

These lounges do more than provide a place to smoke; they cultivate complex social ecosystems where networking, cultural exchange, and personal branding intersect. A conversation over a premium cigar can launch a business deal, forge a professional connection, or simply offer a moment of refined leisure.

The architectural and social design of these spaces reflect broader cultural shifts. In an increasingly digital world, these lounges provide something rare—genuine, face-to-face interaction, where the slow ritual of selecting, cutting, and smoking a cigar offers a counterbalance to the rapid pace of modern communication.

By the second decade of the 21st century, luxury cigar lounges have become more than just venues—they are cultural institutions. Each lounge functions as a microcosm where heritage and innovation, personal pleasure and social performance, coexist in a delicate, fascinating harmony.

Social Media & Online Cigar Communities: Democratizing Expertise

The digital revolution is transforming cigar culture from an exclusive, gatekept tradition into a democratized, globally connected conversation. Social media and online platforms are dismantling the hierarchical structures that once defined tobacco appreciation, creating new spaces for expertise, criticism, and community.

Instagram and YouTube have emerged as powerful visual platforms that are redefining cigar marketing. Influencers and brands no longer simply sell products; they craft entire lifestyle narratives. A single post can transform a boutique cigar brand from an obscure local producer into a global phenomenon. These platforms have turned cigar appreciation into a performative art, where the act of smoking is becoming as important as the tobacco itself.

Platforms like Halfwheel and Cigar Dojo are revolutionizing how consumers evaluate cigars. These websites go beyond simple ratings—they have created sophisticated ecosystems of cigar expertise. Amateur enthusiasts now have access to the same level of detailed information once reserved for industry insiders. Crowd-sourced reviews, detailed tasting notes, and real-time discussions are reshaping how cigars are understood and appreciated.

Virtual cigar communities represent a profound social innovation. Facebook groups and live-streamed "herfs" (virtual cigar gatherings) connect smokers across geographical boundaries. A cigar enthusiast in New York can share a virtual smoking experience with someone in Singapore, exchanging insights, recommendations, and cultural perspectives in real time.

This digital democratization is challenging traditional power structures in the cigar world. Where once expertise was controlled by established magazines and industry veterans, now anyone with passion and a smartphone can contribute to the global conversation. Boutique brands are gaining international recognition without massive marketing budgets, while individual enthusiasts are building personal brands based on genuine expertise and authentic passion.

The algorithmic nature of social media platforms has introduced new marketing dynamics. Hashtags like #CigarLife and #PremiumCigars have become global cultural markers. Brands are discovering that authenticity and storytelling matter more than traditional advertising. A carefully crafted Instagram story can be more powerful than a full-page magazine advertisement.

By the second decade of the 21st century, digital platforms have fundamentally reshaped cigar culture. No longer just communication tools, they are evolving into dynamic cultural spaces where tradition and innovation, expertise and enthusiasm intersect in unprecedented ways.

Today, the digital revolution continues to prove that cigar culture is not just about tobacco—it is about connection, storytelling, and the human desire to share experiences, amplified by technology's unprecedented reach.[11]

WHAT DO THEY SMOKE?

Cigars as Personal Statement

In the boutique era, a cigar is no longer just a tobacco product—it is a personal narrative, a statement of identity. The brands and blends individuals choose reflect not just taste, but personal philosophy, cultural allegiance, and artistic sensibility.

Celebrities and Influencers

• Matt Damon – Damon is often spotted with Drew Estate's Liga Privada, reflecting the boutique brand's appeal to a younger, more sophisticated audience.
• Jay-Z – A passionate cigar enthusiast, Jay-Z is associated with Montecristo and Romeo y Julieta among Cuban brands, and in 2014 launched his own collaboration with General Cigar's Cohiba: the Cohiba Comador, made in the Dominican Republic.
• Joe Rogan – The most influential cigar ambassador of the digital era, Rogan regularly features cigars on his widely popular podcast. With audiences in the tens of millions across YouTube and Spotify, he has effectively transformed cigar appreciation into a mainstream conversation. Known for smoking boutique brands like Tatuaje and Foundation Cigars,

---

[11] It is important to note that the rise of social media marketing in the cigar industry raises important ethical questions about targeting, age verification, and the potential glamorization of tobacco use, particularly among younger audiences.

Rogan turned cigar smoking into a form of long-form, unfiltered media performance.

Entrepreneurs and Business Leaders

• Mark Cuban – A vocal cigar aficionado, Cuban is frequently seen with rare boutique blends, embodying the intersection of technology, entrepreneurship, and cigar culture. Known to enjoy premium brands like Arturo Fuente, Liga Privada, and boutique small-batch cigars.
• Gary Vaynerchuk – Popularized cigar culture among millennials, Vaynerchuk often showcases small-batch and craft cigar brands on his platforms. He has been associated with brands like Oliva and has shown interest in supporting emerging cigar makers.

The Rise of Personal Curation

A new approach to cigar selection emerged—one driven by individuality rather than mass appeal. Smokers are no longer satisfied with generic, factory-produced cigars; instead, they seek unique blends that reflect their personal journey, professional identity, and cultural background.

Cigars have become a form of personal branding—a carefully chosen statement of taste, sophistication, and appreciation for craftsmanship. In the boutique era, what you smoke is just as important as how you smoke it. Celebrities have exemplified such a shift.[12]

Sustainability and Innovation: The Ecological Frontier of Cigar Production

As the boutique cigar movement matures, it confronts a critical challenge that will define its future: how to balance traditional craftsmanship with environmental sustainability and technological innovation. The artisanal approach that revitalized the industry now faces a new imperative—adapting to a rapidly changing global ecosystem.

---

[12] Celebrity cigar preferences often involve complex marketing relationships. While some endorsements are genuine personal preferences, others may involve formal or informal brand partnerships that are not always transparently disclosed.

Tobacco farming has long been an environmental challenge. Traditional growing methods are resource-intensive, often depleting soil and relying on significant chemical inputs. But a new generation of cigar producers is reimagining tobacco cultivation through an ecological lens.

Innovative farms in Nicaragua and the Dominican Republic are experimenting with regenerative agriculture techniques. These approaches go beyond organic farming, focusing on rebuilding soil health, increasing biodiversity, and creating closed-loop agricultural systems. Some producers are implementing carbon-neutral growing practices, using cover crops, minimal tillage, and advanced composting techniques to reduce environmental impact.

Technological innovation is becoming a critical tool in this ecological transformation. Precision agriculture technologies—including drone mapping, soil sensors, and advanced climate monitoring—allow tobacco farmers to optimize growing conditions while minimizing environmental disruption. Machine learning algorithms predict optimal planting times, water usage, and harvest conditions with unprecedented accuracy.

Packaging and distribution represent another frontier of sustainable innovation. Boutique cigar brands are exploring biodegradable packaging, carbon-neutral shipping methods, and transparent supply chain practices. Some companies are offering carbon offset programs, allowing consumers to participate directly in environmental conservation efforts.

The genetic research frontier is opening new possibilities for sustainable tobacco production. Agricultural scientists are developing tobacco strains that are more resistant to climate change, require less water, and can grow in more challenging environments. These efforts aren't just about preserving the industry—they are about reimagining tobacco as a potentially regenerative agricultural product.

This ecological approach is more than just an environmental strategy; it represents a fundamental shift in how cigars are perceived. No longer merely luxury indulgences, they are becoming symbols of sustainable craftsmanship—deeply connected to agricultural innovation, environmental stewardship, and the evolving global marketplace.

As the cigar industry moves deeper into the 21st century, it stands at a pivotal moment. The boutique movement has already proven that tradition and innovation can coexist. Now, it must demonstrate that sustainability and craftsmanship are not opposing forces but essential partners in shaping the future of premium cigars.

The Boutique Cigar: A Cultural Reimagining

The boutique cigar renaissance represents more than a market trend—it is a fundamental shift in how cigars are conceived, produced, and appreciated. Small, independent brands are redefining the very essence of cigar craftsmanship.[13]

This movement is ushering in a new era of creativity and experimentation. Boutique manufacturers are transforming blending and fermentation techniques, breaking away from the standardized formulas that long dominated the industry. By exploring rare tobacco varietals, adjusting fermentation times, and fine-tuning aging methods, they are creating cigars with a depth and complexity that set them apart.

Beyond production, boutique cigars are reshaping consumer expectations. Smokers no longer seek only familiar brands; they pursue cigars that offer distinctive flavor profiles, limited availability, and artisanal excellence. This shift has made boutique cigars a symbol of connoisseurship, appealing to those who value craftsmanship over mass production.

The rise of boutique cigars is also influencing the broader industry. Larger manufacturers have taken notice, incorporating elements of boutique innovation into their own lines. Legacy brands are experimenting with

---

[13] The boutique cigar movement emerged within a complex regulatory landscape, which we will explore in the next chapter. The FDA's 2016 deeming rule sought to impose strict testing and pre-market approval requirements, posing significant challenges for small manufacturers. However, these regulations were ultimately overturned in January 2025, removing major barriers that could have stifled the growth of boutique brands.

small-batch releases, vintage tobaccos, and more transparent storytelling to compete with the growing demand for authenticity.

By the mid-2020s, boutique cigars are no longer an industry outlier; they have become a dominant force in shaping modern cigar culture. The movement proves that cigars are more than luxury products—they are expressions of artistry, tradition, and relentless innovation.

The Economics of Boutique Cigar Production: Reimagining Market Dynamics

The boutique cigar movement represents more than an artistic revolution—it is a fundamental reimagining of tobacco economics. Where large manufacturers have prioritized volume and consistency, boutique brands have introduced a radically different economic model based on scarcity, craftsmanship, and storytelling.

Pricing Strategies: Beyond Commodity

Traditional cigar pricing had been relatively straightforward—based on production costs, tobacco quality, and market demand. Boutique brands have transformed this equation. A $25 boutique cigar in the early 2020s is no longer just a product but an experience, a collector's item, and a narrative unto itself. Some brands intentionally limit production runs, creating a sense of exclusivity that drives prices upward.

Take Drew Estate's Liga Privada line, for instance. Initially created as a private blend for the company's employees, its limited availability and exceptional quality turned it into a cult phenomenon. Prices that would have been unthinkable a decade earlier became not just acceptable but desirable among serious enthusiasts.

Challenges for Small Manufacturers

The economic barriers to entry in the cigar industry remain formidable. Boutique brands face significant challenges:

- High initial capital requirements for quality tobacco
- Complex regulatory environments
- Limited distribution channels
- Competition from established brands
- Significant aging and production costs

Many boutique brands have survived through innovative strategies. Some have formed cooperative purchasing agreements, sharing resources and distribution channels. Others have developed direct-to-consumer models through online platforms and social media, bypassing traditional wholesale networks.

Market Dynamics and Consumer Transformation

The boutique movement has fundamentally altered consumer expectations. Where previous generations viewed cigars as a luxury commodity, new consumers see them as artisanal products. This shift allows smaller manufacturers to compete directly with industry giants by emphasizing unique narratives, transparent production methods, and exceptional craftsmanship.

Brands like Warped Cigars and Illusione demonstrate that scale isn't dictated by quality. By focusing on limited, meticulously crafted productions, these companies have created market niches that larger manufacturers can't easily replicate.

The economic model of boutique cigar production reflects a broader trend in consumer culture, as we've seen—a move from mass production to artisanal, story-driven consumption. It is an approach that values individual expression over uniformity, complexity over simplicity.

Cigar Aging and Blending Techniques: The Science and Art of Tobacco Transformation

In the world of boutique cigars, blending and aging have been elevated from industrial processes to complex artistic expressions. Each cigar has become a carefully composed symphony of tobacco, with blenders acting as maestros orchestrating intricate flavor profiles.

The Science of Tobacco Blending

Modern blending techniques represent a sophisticated intersection of agricultural science, sensory analysis, and creative intuition. Blenders no longer simply combine tobaccos—they conduct intricate experiments in flavor, combustion, and sensory experience.

Tobacco selection has evolved into a meticulous science. Blenders consider not just the origin of each leaf but its specific microclimate, soil composition, and genetic lineage. A Nicaraguan Jalapa Valley ligero might be paired with a Dominican Piloto Cubano seco to create a complex flavor architecture that tells a specific narrative.

Advanced Aging Methodologies

Aging has transformed from a passive storage process to an active flavor development technique. Some boutique manufacturers have begun experimenting with:
• Controlled humidity environments
• Specific wood-lined aging rooms
• Precise temperature and moisture management
• Extended aging periods spanning multiple years

Brands like Padrón demonstrate how aging can transform tobacco. Their Anniversary series cigars are aged for years, allowing flavors to mellow and integrate in ways that defy traditional production timelines.

The Art of Sensory Composition

Blending has become a form of culinary composition. Blenders speak of tobacco leaves like chefs discussing ingredients—considering not just individual flavors, but how different tobaccos interact, complement, and challenge each other.

A truly exceptional blend requires understanding tobacco's most subtle characteristics. The spicy note of a Nicaraguan ligero, the creamy smoothness of a Connecticut shade wrapper, the earthy undertones of a Honduran binder—these are not just ingredients but musical notes in a complex sensory composition.

Technological Innovation in Blending

Advanced technologies have begun to transform blending techniques. Spectral analysis, molecular flavor profiling, and computer modeling allow blenders to predict and manipulate tobacco interactions with unprecedented precision.

Yet, for all the scientific advancement, the best blenders understand that true artistry resides in intuition, in that ineffable moment where technical knowledge meets creative vision.

Conclusion: The Future of the Boutique Cigar Movement

The boutique cigar renaissance has proven that cigars are not relics of the past but a continuously evolving craft, driven by innovation, artistry, and a renewed commitment to quality. This movement has reshaped consumer expectations, demonstrating that small, independent brands can produce cigars rivaling—or even surpassing—those of the industry's longest-standing giants.

As American-grown tobacco experiences a resurgence, luxury cigar lounges redefine social rituals, and digital platforms foster a new global community of enthusiasts, the cigar industry stands at the intersection of tradition and reinvention. The same patience and craftsmanship that define a fine cigar also define the industry's future—one that embraces both heritage and innovation, ensuring that the art of cigar-making continues to thrive for generations to come.

"The FDA's regulation of premium cigars
was arbitrary and capricious."

— U.S. Court of Appeals for the D.C. Circuit,
Cigar Association of America v. FDA, January 24, 2025

———

In a single ruling, a decade of regulatory threat collapsed. The premium cigar industry—small, artisanal, and economically marginal—had won a constitutional victory that reshaped its future. Chapter 7 begins where the law left off: with an industry suddenly free to imagine what comes next.

CHAPTER 7

The Future of the Cigar Industry

Globalization in overdrive | The late 20ᵗʰ and early 21ˢᵗ centuries ushered in an era of unprecedented global connectivity, dismantling barriers between cultures, reshaping economies, and redefining identity on a scale never seen before. Ideas, products, and traditions are no longer confined by geography; they now move instantly and in multiple directions, blending cultures, intertwining economies, and shaping individual identities through both local heritage and global influence.

This is not merely an economic phenomenon. Globalization today is a lived experience—one driven by digital technologies, cultural hybridization, and a redefinition of expertise, creativity, and consumption. It is a paradoxical force that expands cultural exchange while simultaneously intensifying efforts to preserve local identity, ensuring that tradition and innovation evolve together in an increasingly interconnected world.

The Digital Revolution as a Catalyst

At the heart of this transformation is the internet, which has reshaped globalization from a slow-moving economic trend into an instantaneous and interactive experience. Unlike previous eras of global trade and migration, where influence flowed primarily from industrialized nations outward, today's digital age has made culture, commerce, and information borderless.

Social media platforms, streaming services, and digital communication tools collapsed geographical distances, forging new communities where cultural exchange is constant. A consumer in Paris can purchase handcrafted cigars from Nicaragua after watching a YouTube review from a cigar aficionado in New York, while a rapper in Lagos can build a global following without ever signing with a Western record label.

These shifts have radically altered how people engage with expertise, identity, and tradition. Knowledge is no longer dictated by academic institutions or industry gatekeepers. Instead, YouTube tutorials, online forums, and social networks allow enthusiasts to develop deep expertise, whether in cigars, bourbon, fashion, or any other specialized craft. The rise of networked individualism— a concept coined by sociologists and media theorists—describes this new world, where individuals can form global knowledge networks and communities based on shared passions, rather than shared geography.

Cultural Hybridization and Identity in the Global Era

As the world has become more connected, traditional cultural boundaries have blurred, giving rise to new forms of hybrid identity. People today construct identities that are both deeply local and unmistakably global, seamlessly blending traditions from multiple cultures.

Music provides a perfect example. K-pop, originally a distinctly South Korean genre, has become a global force, with fans worldwide embracing Korean cultural references, and engaging in transnational fan communities. The same can be seen in streetwear, where Japanese aesthetics, American hip-hop culture, and European high fashion collide to create something wholly new. Fusion cuisine, too, reflects this global blending, where a restaurant in São Paulo might serve Japanese-Brazilian dishes, and a New York chef might reinterpret Korean barbecue with locally sourced ingredients.

The global exchange of traditions has not erased cultural distinctions but reshaped them. Cigar culture, like music and fashion, is evolving into a fusion of influences—where a lounge in Shanghai may cater to a European clientele, and a boutique brand in Miami sources tobacco from four continents.

Bourbon, Cigars, and the Globalization of Taste

In today's globalized world, products are no longer merely goods—they have evolved into expressions of identity, heritage, and artistry. This cultural shift is particularly evident in the world of premium cigars. By maintaining a continuous parallel with bourbon, we gain a deeper appreciation for quality, craftsmanship, and tradition—elements that have transcended regional boundaries to shape a truly global connoisseurship.

Once deeply rooted in specific regions, both cigars and bourbon have undergone a dramatic transformation driven by globalization. American bourbon, once overshadowed by Scotch whisky, has surged in popularity across the globe. Distillers such as Woodford Reserve and Angel's Envy have redefined what it means to produce premium spirits, embracing small-batch production, experimental aging, and the revival of historic recipes. This shift is not confined to the United States; craft bourbon has become increasingly popular in Europe, China, and India, regions where the taste for high-quality, artisanal spirits is on the rise.

Similarly, the world of premium cigars has entered a new era of cultural appreciation. Enthusiasts are no longer just reaching for well-known Cuban brands—instead, they are seeking boutique blends from Nicaragua, Honduras, the Dominican Republic, as well as all-American boutique cigars. Much like bourbon, cigars have been shifting from mass production to a focus on terroir, craftsmanship, and exclusivity. The rise of artisanal cigars mirrors the growing demand for small-batch spirits, single-origin coffee, and handcrafted chocolates—luxury items that prioritize quality over quantity.

As this shift continues, the experience of consuming premium boutique cigars, just like craft bourbon, has become just as important as the product itself. These aren't merely indulgences; they are rituals, storytelling devices, and symbols of connoisseurship. Modern enthusiasts aren't just smoking a cigar or sipping a whiskey—they are engaging with the history, tradition, and artistry that have shaped these fine products over generations.

For those who appreciate the finer things in life, boutique cigars have become part of a broader cultural movement that celebrates craftsmanship, regional heritage, and the deep connection between producer and consumer. This movement is not just about enjoying high-quality products—it's about savoring the stories behind them, the legacy of the artisans who make them, and the global community that shares in their appreciation.

The Democratization of Expertise and the Evolution of Luxury

Traditionally, expertise in cigars, spirits, and luxury goods was shaped by a small group of insiders—industry professionals, critics, and high-end retailers who dictated trends. But in the digital age, expertise has become more democratized than ever before.

Online platforms like Reddit, Instagram, YouTube, and specialized cigar forums have turned consumers into participants in the luxury market, rather than passive buyers. A cigar enthusiast no longer needs access to exclusive lounges or industry insiders to develop knowledge; they can explore cigar-making regions virtually, read direct accounts from master blenders, and discover rare, boutique releases from around the world—all from their smartphone.

The same holds true for bourbon, wine, watches, and bespoke fashion. The modern connoisseur is just as likely to have gained their expertise from a deep dive into digital knowledge networks as from traditional high-end retail experiences. This shift has led to a new kind of luxury consumer— one who values authenticity, craftsmanship, and story over mere prestige.

The Paradox of Globalization: Expansion and Preservation

As discussed earlier, globalization's rapid expansion has not erased local identity—if anything, it has strengthened the desire to preserve and celebrate unique traditions. While embracing global influences, people are also reclaiming and redefining their cultural heritage.

This paradox is visible in cigar production, where the growing international market has fueled interest in regional tobaccos, historical fermentation techniques, and small-scale production methods. Rather than making cigars a generic global product, globalization has made them more nuanced, specialized, and regionally expressive.

Similarly, as bourbon became a global luxury product, it inspired American distillers to look backward to move forward—resurrecting pre-Prohibition recipes, experimenting with heirloom grains, and refining barrel-aging techniques that had been forgotten in the rush toward mass production.

Rather than a monolithic, one-size-fits-all culture, today's world is defined by a complex interplay of tradition and innovation, local heritage and global exchange.

The Future of Globalized Craftsmanship

Globalization in the digital era is not about uniformity—it is about complexity, interconnectedness, and reinvention. The 21st-century world has dissolved borders, reshaped cultural identity, and transformed how people engage with knowledge, expertise, and luxury.

Globalization has expanded—not erased—cigar craftsmanship. Instead of homogenizing products, it has amplified niche markets. Consumers now seek cigars that emphasize regional heritage, and master blenders incorporate tobaccos from multiple terroirs to create entirely new flavor profiles.

But while globalization has expanded appreciation for craftsmanship, cigars now stand at a crossroads. The same forces fueling a revival in small-batch artistry—rising consumer expectations, digital communities, and a passion for authenticity—are now clashing with growing government regulations, shifting global markets, and uncertain industry dynamics. The future of cigars, once shaped solely by connoisseurs and master blenders, is now increasingly influenced, perhaps detrimentally, by policymakers, emerging economies, and shifting consumer habits.

America's Cigar: A Legacy in Transition

For more than 250 years, cigars have remained a defining thread in America's cultural and economic landscape. From the tobacco fields of colonial Virginia to the cigar factories of 19th-century New York and the exclusive lounges of today, they have adapted through eras of social, political, and economic change. More than a luxury, cigars have symbolized power, craftsmanship, defiance, and tradition.

But today, the cigar industry stands at a crossroads. The forces shaping its future are unlike anything it has faced before: growing government regulations, shifting global markets, advances in blending and fermentation, and the rise of digital technology. Will cigars continue their legacy as a refined luxury product, or will increasing restrictions attempt to push them into obscurity?

While some see a future fraught with challenges, others believe the best days of cigars are yet to come. The following pages explore the key forces shaping the modern cigar world—the regulatory battles, the rise of new global markets, technological innovations, and the evolving preferences of cigar smokers in the 21st century.

The Battle Against Regulation: Cigars vs. the FDA

In the quiet, wood-paneled back rooms of cigar lounges across America, a different kind of war was being waged—one that had escalated in the early 21st century. This battle didn't involve tobacco fields or trade routes but played out in courtrooms and regulatory hearing chambers. The enemy was not a competing nation or a market shift but a government agency expanding its regulatory reach.

The Food and Drug Administration's 2016 decision landed like a thunderbolt in the cigar world. What had been a nuanced, artisanal craft was suddenly being treated like a mass-produced health hazard. Bureaucrats in Washington seemed to see no difference between a machine-rolled cigarette and a carefully crafted, small-batch cigar hand-rolled by a master artisan with generations of family tradition.

The regulatory framework imposed was more than a bureaucratic inconvenience—it was an existential threat. Each new cigar blend would now require a review process that could cost hundreds of thousands of dollars and take over a year to complete. For boutique manufacturers operating on razor-thin margins, this was equivalent to a death sentence. Small brands that had been pushing the boundaries of blending and craftsmanship found themselves facing potential extinction.

The regulations weren't just about pre-market approvals. They touched every aspect of the business—marketing restrictions that made it nearly impossible to tell the story behind a cigar, packaging limitations that stripped away brand identity, and taxation structures that threatened to price artisanal cigars out of existence.

The industry's response was a testament to the passion that drives cigar culture. It wasn't just about business; it was about preserving a craft, a tradition that stretched back generations. The Premium Cigar Association (PCA) mounted legal challenges, arguing that premium cigars were fundamentally different from mass-market tobacco products. These were not disposable commodities, but carefully crafted expressions of agricultural art.

A significant breakthrough came in 2022 when a federal judge ruled that the FDA had acted arbitrarily in its approach to premium cigars.[14] It was a temporary victory then, but one that highlighted the fundamental misunderstanding at the heart of the regulatory approach. How could an

---

[14] On July 5, 2022, Judge Amit P. Mehta of the U.S. District Court for the District of Columbia ruled that the FDA acted arbitrarily and capriciously in its decision not to exempt premium cigars from the Deeming Rule. This ruling was further solidified on August 9, 2023, when the same court vacated the FDA's regulation of premium cigars, effectively removing them from the FDA's regulatory authority. The FDA appealed this decision, but on January 24, 2025, the U.S. Court of Appeals for the District of Columbia Circuit upheld the district court's ruling, agreeing that the FDA's regulation of premium cigars was indeed arbitrary and capricious.

agency designed to protect public health fail to distinguish between a mass-produced cigarette and a cigar that might be enjoyed once a month, never inhaled, part of a rich cultural tradition?

The battle was about more than economics—it was about cultural preservation. Each regulation threatened to flatten the rich, nuanced world of cigar craftsmanship into a uniform, sanitized version of itself. The stakes were nothing less than the survival of an art form—a delicate ecosystem of farmers, blenders, rollers, and enthusiasts who had spent generations perfecting their craft.

That fight was set to potentially continue for years, but in 2025, the industry secured its most significant victory yet.

The Industry's Landmark Win Against FDA Regulation

In a pivotal moment for the premium cigar industry, the United States Court of Appeals for the D.C. Circuit delivered a landmark ruling in January 2025 that affirmed a lower-court ruling vacating the FDA's deeming rule as applied to premium cigars. This decision was the culmination of years of legal battles, scientific debates, and a nuanced understanding of artisanal tobacco production. The case has been remanded for further refinement, and the FDA retains authority to pursue new rulemaking, but for now premium cigars sit outside the deeming framework.

The case represented more than a legal dispute—it was a profound examination of how regulatory agencies define and categorize tobacco products. Premium cigars, crafted through generations of expertise, had long been lumped together with mass-produced tobacco products, despite fundamentally different production methods, consumption patterns, and cultural significance.

The appeals court's ruling was a comprehensive rejection of the FDA's regulatory approach. Judges meticulously examined evidence demonstrating that premium cigars—typically hand-rolled, made with select tobacco, and consumed in distinctly different contexts from mass-market cigarettes—warranted a unique regulatory perspective. The decision highlighted the artisanal nature of premium cigars, recognizing them as a craft product with deep cultural roots rather than a standardized consumer good.

Industry representatives argued that the ruling validated their long-standing position: premium cigars are a distinctive craft product that requires a tailored regulatory approach. Their argument centered on the fundamental difference between artisanal cigar production and mass-market tobacco products, emphasizing that effective regulation should reflect the unique characteristics and consumption patterns of premium cigars. The decision eliminated several existential regulatory threats:
• Costly pre-market tobacco product applications
• Extensive testing and documentation requirements
• Severe marketing restrictions
• Potential flavor and blend limitations

For small manufacturers and boutique brands—many of which are family-owned businesses with generations of expertise—the ruling was nothing short of transformative. The compliance requirements had threatened to transform a centuries-old craft into a bureaucratic nightmare, potentially driving numerous artisanal producers out of business. [15]

Beyond the immediate legal victory, the ruling represented a broader recognition of craftsmanship in an era of increasing industrialization. It acknowledged that some products are more than mere commodities—they are living traditions, cultural artifacts passed down through generations of skilled artisans.

But regulatory landscapes are never permanently settled. The challenge ahead would be to continue demonstrating the unique value of premium cigars: not just as a product, but as a sophisticated craft with deep cultural significance.

---

[15] Notwithstanding its potential impact on the consumer market, the FDA's regulatory approach would have disproportionately affected the remaining premium handmade cigar manufacturers in the United States. In Miami, small-batch, handcrafted production continues at operations like El Titan de Bronze, Cuba Tobacco Cigar Co., and many others. J.C. Newman Cigar Co. in Tampa remains the last major factory producing both handmade and machine-made cigars. Meanwhile, Pennsylvania remains a hub for large-scale, machine-made production, with companies such as John Middleton Co. and Altadis USA focused on mass-market cigars. The ruling recognized that premium cigars are fundamentally different from mass-produced tobacco products, thus preventing regulations that could have driven small-scale, artisanal manufacturers out of business.

Beyond Traditional Boundaries

In the wake of the landmark January 2025 court ruling that vacated the FDA's deeming rule as applied to premium cigars—only recently as of this book's publication—the industry finds itself at a pivotal moment of transformation. This legal victory is more than just a regulatory reprieve; it has ushered in a renewed focus on broader shifts in global tobacco consumption.

The industry's evolution is not only geographic—it is also demographic. The modern cigar landscape is being shaped by a more diverse range of consumers, challenging long-held assumptions about who smokes cigars and why. Women, once overlooked in traditional cigar marketing, are now a visible and growing segment, bringing new energy to both luxury branding and social cigar culture. Similarly, Black cigar smokers have emerged as a driving force in the boutique and premium markets, reclaiming a cultural legacy that stretches back generations.

These shifts are not happening in isolation. They reflect a broader redefinition of cigar culture, one that embraces inclusivity while maintaining the craftsmanship and prestige that have long defined the industry. As the U.S. market diversifies, the global stage is also evolving, with rising economies like China, India, and the Middle East shaping the next chapter of cigar consumption.

The Rise of Women in the Cigar Industry

The cigar industry has experienced a cultural transformation in recent years, with a noticeable shift toward greater inclusivity and recognition of women as key consumers. This change is reflected in a growing number of campaigns that target women, not only as consumers of luxury cigars but also as symbols of sophistication, empowerment, and luxury. Increasingly, cigar brands have featured women in their advertisements, moving away from traditional portrayals of cigars as symbols of masculinity and male-dominated leisure.

Throughout the 2010s, several campaigns helped redefine the cigar experience, framing it as an indulgence accessible to both men and women. Advertisements showcasing women in luxurious settings enjoying cigars began to highlight feminine strength, elegance, and cultural status, positioning cigars as a symbol of personal empowerment and luxury for all. For instance, Rocky Patel's Prohibition campaign, featuring Jessica Tyann, emphasized cigars as a luxury product for women who appreciate not only craftsmanship but also the cultural significance that cigars symbolize. This shift was part of a larger industry-wide movement to appeal to a growing female demographic.

Rocky Patel Prohibition Campaign (2010s). Featuring Jessica Tyann Crovato. This ad breaks traditional gender norms in cigar marketing, highlighting women as discerning consumers of luxury cigars. The campaign redefines cigars as a symbol of sophistication and empowerment for women, mirroring the broader trend of inclusivity in the luxury market.

This cultural shift also mirrors broader trends in the luxury market, particularly in industries such as craft bourbon and artisanal goods. Across Europe, China, and India, women are increasingly embracing products that emphasize personal identity, empowerment, and refinement. Much like how craft bourbon brands have tailored their offerings to appeal to women—focusing on small-batch production and heritage—cigar brands have adjusted their marketing strategies to embrace these values as well.

As the global cigar market expands, the rise of boutique cigars has played a significant role in this shift. Today, cigars are seen as symbols of cultural appreciation and luxury that transcend traditional gender roles. This evolution reflects a broader democratization of the cigar-smoking experience, one where both men and women are celebrated as active participants in the world of premium cigars and fine spirits.

This transformation is helping to redefine the cigar industry, paving the way for a more inclusive and diverse luxury market. Brands like Rocky Patel and Cohiba Red Dot have embraced these shifts, helping to open doors for women to be seen not only as consumers but also as innovators and leaders in the cigar world. Boutique brands like Tres Lindas Cubanas Cigars, founded by Afro-Cuban twin sisters Yvette and Yvonne Rodriguez, and Noble Cigars, led by Elizabeth Santos, exemplify this shift—demonstrating that women are not merely participants but leading innovators in the industry. Their success marks a turning point where traditional gender roles are increasingly left behind, making way for a dynamic and inclusive global market.

As women continue to reshape the cigar industry, another historically overlooked group has also played a crucial role in its evolution. Black cigar smokers, entrepreneurs, and collectors have long contributed to the culture and business of premium cigars, yet their influence has often been underrepresented in mainstream narratives.

Inclusion and Heritage: The Role of Black Communities in Cigar Culture

While the cigar industry has often been associated with certain iconic regions and demographics, it's essential to recognize the influence of Black communities in shaping modern cigar culture. From the establishment of cigar lounges to the rise of Black cigar enthusiasts and collectors, these communities have long been part of the fabric of cigar culture, both as consumers and tastemakers.

In recent years, Black entrepreneurs and brands have made a significant impact on the premium cigar industry, driving greater diversity and inclusivity while redefining the social and cultural dimensions of cigar smoking. Brands like Black Star Line Cigars, founded by Aric Bey, and Emperors Cut Cigars, known for its "Jazz Series," have gained recognition for their high-quality blends and commitment to craftsmanship. These companies, along with influential figures in the industry, have helped expand cigar culture beyond the product itself, embracing elements of lifestyle, identity, and community. As the global cigar industry continues to evolve, the contributions of Black entrepreneurs and enthusiasts are playing an essential role in shaping the future of premium cigars through innovation, authenticity, and a deep respect for tradition.

As the cigar industry embraces a more diverse consumer base, these cultural shifts are not confined to the United States. Around the world, emerging markets are redefining the landscape of premium cigars, with new regions and economies stepping into the spotlight.

The Expanding Global Landscape of Cigar Culture

The traditional centers of cigar production and consumption are being challenged, replaced by a more dynamic, globally interconnected landscape. Where once the industry was dominated by established markets in the United States, the Caribbean, and Western Europe, a new generation of cigar enthusiasts was rising in regions previously overlooked.

China: The New Epicenter of Cigar Culture?

In the gleaming high-rises of Shanghai and Beijing, a remarkable transformation has reshaped the global cigar landscape. What began as a strategic push into Asian markets has evolved into an unprecedented success story. China has emerged as the world's largest market for Cuban cigars by value, a shift that has taken place gradually over the past decade, particularly from the mid-2010s to early 2020s. This transformation reflects not only significant growth in demand but also a redefined perception of cigars within China's affluent consumer base. The rise of luxury consumption, paired with strategic marketing by Habanos S.A., has cultivated a sophisticated market that now rivals traditional cigar powerhouses like the United States.[16]

Even amid global economic uncertainty, China's appetite for premium cigars has only intensified. In 2020, sales of Cuban cigars in the country surged by 15 percent, highlighting the increasing role of cigars as both a luxury indulgence and a status symbol. Since 2012, Habanos S.A. has refined its marketing approach to target China's elite consumers, launching limited editions and regional releases that often incorporate Chinese cultural elements.

Beyond consumption, China has introduced a new paradigm in cigar collecting. Unlike traditional markets where cigars are primarily smoked, many Chinese consumers view them as investment assets—on par with fine wines and rare artifacts. Exclusive releases often appreciate in value within months, creating a dynamic secondary market that mirrors China's broader luxury goods ecosystem.

This shift has also transformed China's cigar lounges into more than just smoking venues. In major cities, high-end cigar lounges have become hubs for investment discussions, cultural exchanges, and elite networking. These establishments offer curated vintage collections, expert-led tastings, and exclusive events, elevating cigars as an integral part of China's luxury lifestyle.

The growing sophistication of China's cigar market has pushed manufacturers to innovate, from blend development to packaging design, to meet the expectations of this influential demographic. The impact of

---

[16] However, it's important to note that while China has surpassed other regions in Cuban cigar sales, the United States remains the largest market overall for premium cigars, including both Cuban and non-Cuban brands in other markets. Despite the Cuban Embargo—which has kept Cuban cigars largely out of U.S. markets—the American market continues to dominate premium cigar consumption. U.S. consumers, who have long favored brands from countries like Nicaragua, Honduras, and the Dominican Republic, continue to be a driving force in the global cigar industry.

China's rise is reflected in global pricing trends and the international price homogenization policies that have emerged to accommodate this powerful consumer base.

Looking ahead, industry analysts project continued growth in this vital market, with the luxury cigar sector expected to reach USD 10.5 billion by 2034. This growth represents more than just economic success—it signals the continued evolution of cigar culture, where Eastern and Western traditions merge to create new patterns of appreciation and consumption.

For the global cigar industry, China represents more than just a market—it's a glimpse into the future of premium tobacco appreciation, where tradition meets innovation, and where the art of cigar making finds new expressions in an ancient culture.

India: The Emerging Luxury Landscape

India's relationship with cigars tells a story of economic transformation. As the country's middle class expanded in the early 2000s, so did its appetite for luxury experiences. By the 2010s, premium cigar consumption had grown significantly, driven by increasing disposable income and a rising number of affluent professionals. Despite historically strict tobacco regulations, high-end cigar lounges began appearing in Mumbai, Delhi, and Bangalore, catering to a niche but steadily expanding market.

These weren't just smoking spaces—they were cultural institutions. By the mid-2010s, exclusive members-only lounges like The Cigar Lounge at The Oberoi in Mumbai and The Smoke Company in Bangalore redefined the cigar experience. These venues offered more than just a place to smoke; they provided curated experiences, from sommelier-guided pairings to rare whiskey collections, creating an atmosphere where business and leisure seamlessly intersected.

For India's emerging professional class, a fine cigar is a statement of success, sophistication, and cultural refinement. While challenges such as high import duties on cigars persist, India's role in the global cigar market continues to evolve, with an increasing number of connoisseurs embracing the luxury and heritage of premium cigars.

The Middle East: Opulence Meets Tradition

By the early 2000s, the Middle East had emerged as a powerhouse in the global luxury market, and premium cigars were no exception. In cities like Dubai, Doha, and Abu Dhabi, cigars became a performance of wealth and sophistication. Five-star hotels and private clubs competed to create the most exclusive cigar lounges, catering to an elite clientele that viewed smoking as both a ritual and a status symbol.

By the mid-2010s, iconic venues such as the Churchill Lounge at the Four Seasons in Dubai and The Cigar Lounge at the St. Regis in Abu Dhabi became hubs for connoisseurs and business elites alike. These establishments didn't just offer cigars; they curated collections of rare and vintage smokes, elevating the cigar experience to a new level of indulgence.

The region's demand for Cuban cigars was insatiable. With the U.S. embargo restricting access to Cuban brands for American consumers, Middle Eastern buyers became dominant players in the global cigar trade. By the late 2010s, wealthy collectors in the Gulf were spending hundreds of thousands of dollars on vintage Cuban cigars, treating them as investment assets on par with fine art and rare whiskey.

As the Middle East continues to embrace luxury culture, its role in shaping global cigar trends is undeniable. The region remains a key market for exclusive releases, high-end lounges, and some of the world's most extravagant cigar experiences.

Europe: A Cornerstone of the Global Cigar Market

As new markets in China, India, and the Middle East surge, Europe continues to occupy a central seat at the table in the evolving global cigar landscape. While the rise of these emerging economies has shifted the focus of the cigar industry in recent years, Europe's long-standing legacy in cigar consumption and culture remains a defining force shaping the future of the industry. Geographically and economically speaking, Europe encompasses a diverse and sophisticated cigar culture that spans from the traditional heartlands of Spain and Switzerland to Eastern Europe's emerging luxury markets, as well as the more niche yet dedicated cigar communities in Scandinavia.

Europe has historically been both a cultural hub and a key market for cigars, particularly Cuban varieties, which hold a revered status across the continent. Countries like France, Germany, Switzerland, and the United Kingdom have long been essential to the success of premium cigar brands. European enthusiasts' appreciation for craftsmanship and luxury has driven demand for cigars and influenced cigar production worldwide. Even in Scandinavia, where high tobacco taxes and strict regulations have limited mass-market growth, a strong cigar culture persists. Denmark, in particular, has a deep-rooted tobacco tradition, with Copenhagen home to some of Northern Europe's most respected cigar retailers. Meanwhile, Sweden and Norway host exclusive cigar lounges catering to high-end clientele, offering curated pairings with regional spirits like aquavit and fine whisky

This enduring relationship underscores Europe's importance not only as a major consumer market but as a leading tastemaker in the luxury goods industry. Whether through its historic cigar-producing regions or its evolving boutique scene, the continent remains a key player in shaping the global cigar market.

In addition to being a major consumer, Europe also remains influential in the branding and innovation of premium cigars. European hubs of premium cigar blending and distribution, such as Switzerland and Spain, house some of the most respected brands in the industry, such as Davidoff and José L. Piedra. These brands emphasize the importance of quality craftsmanship, using both traditional and modern techniques to produce cigars that cater to the tastes of discerning consumers globally. This blend of heritage and innovation keeps European cigars in demand and positions them as luxury items with both historic roots and modern appeal.

In the past decade, Eastern Europe has also become an integral player in the growing global luxury market, with a rising appetite for fine cigars in countries such as Poland, Hungary and Russia. The expansion of high-end cigar lounges in cities like Moscow, Warsaw, and Bucharest is a testament to how Europe's premium cigar culture is evolving, appealing to a new class of affluent professionals seeking sophisticated experiences. These consumers see cigars as symbols of success and distinction—integral parts of a luxurious lifestyle that includes rare whiskies, vintage wines, and fine dining.

Simultaneously, Europe continues to be a vital hub for luxury cigar events and cigar tourism, drawing enthusiasts from around the world. From Davidoff's heritage in Geneva to the cigar-tasting culture of Madrid and Barcelona, Europe hosts both established lounges and rotating events that showcase the art of cigar making and the refined nature of the experience. These venues not only offer consumers the opportunity to enjoy cigars in the most elegant settings, but also serve as cultural gathering points where the exchange of ideas and the appreciation of premium craftsmanship are central to the cigar experience.

Looking to the future, the role of Europe in the global cigar market remains secure, though evolving. The continent is embracing sustainability and ethical consumption, with increasing demand for cigars produced with environmentally conscious practices. European consumers are increasingly seeking transparency regarding the social and environmental impact of tobacco farming, which is pushing boutique brands to tell compelling stories of sustainability while continuing to meet the high expectations of quality. This aligns with a broader luxury trend where craftsmanship and heritage are valued just as much as the story behind the product.

As global markets diversify, Europe will remain a pivotal player in shaping the future of the cigar industry. The region's unique blend of historic expertise, cultural significance, and innovative practices ensures that Europe will continue to be a key influence on the evolving definition of luxury cigars. While new markets in China, India, and the Middle East bring fresh opportunities, Europe's position as a global leader in both consumer demand and branding cements its role as an essential force in the international cigar market.

A Global Transformation

What has emerged is not just a new set of markets but a fundamental reimagining of cigar culture. No longer is this a story of American or Cuban dominance. This is a global narrative—one where tradition meets innovation and local cultures reinterpret a centuries-old practice.

As cigar culture evolves, so too do the dynamics of both production and consumption. On the production side, Brazil and Mexico—both steeped in tobacco heritage—continue to shape the premium cigar landscape. Beyond the established manufacturing centers of the Dominican Republic, Nicaragua, and Honduras, Brazil's Mata Fina tobacco is prized for its distinctive sweetness, while Mexico's San Andrés wrapper remains a cornerstone of premium blends. Meanwhile, on the consumer side, luxury markets in Mexico, Argentina, and Brazil are fueling demand for high-end cigars, with elite lounges in Mexico City, São Paulo, and Buenos Aires catering to a refined and discerning clientele.

The cigar is becoming something new—a global product that speaks different languages, tells different stories, but still maintains its core essence of craftsmanship and experience.

What does it mean for the American cigar industry?

This global transformation represents both a challenge and an opportunity for the U.S. cigar industry. The domestic market, long considered the traditional heartland of premium cigars, now finds itself competing in a rapidly evolving global landscape. Manufacturers must adapt, developing new blends, marketing strategies, and distribution channels that can compete on an international stage. The January 2025 court ruling has not just preserved the industry's regulatory breathing room, but has potentially positioned American cigar makers to become key players in this new global market. Innovation, once a hallmark of boutique American producers, is now their most critical asset in maintaining relevance in a world where cigar culture is being redefined from Shanghai to Dubai.

As competition intensifies, the quest for differentiation has driven cigar makers toward deeper innovation—not just in branding and distribution, but in the very essence of what makes a cigar unique.

Innovation in Blending & Fermentation: The Alchemists of Tobacco

In the quiet, humidity-controlled rooms where master blenders work, a quiet revolution is unfolding. Innovation is creating a renaissance of flavor, technique, and possibility.

The art of cigar making had always been part science, part magic. Now, it has become something entirely new—a complex dialogue between agricultural expertise, chemical understanding, and pure creative vision. Tobacco is no longer just a crop; it is a canvas for unprecedented experimentation.

Hybrid tobacco strains have emerged as the first frontier of innovation. Today, geneticists and master growers continue to treat tobacco like a sophisticated culinary ingredient, crossbreeding plants to create flavor profiles that would have been unimaginable a generation earlier. A tobacco leaf is no longer just a leaf—it is a carefully engineered expression of agricultural art.

Some of the most radical experiments have occurred in fermentation. Traditional aging processes, which had remained largely unchanged for centuries, are being completely reimagined. Cigars are now aged in bourbon barrels, creating complex flavor interactions that blur the lines between tobacco and spirits. Underground cellars have become laboratories where time itself seems to be an ingredient, with some manufacturers experimenting with aging processes that stretch over decades.

As cigar makers push the boundaries of blending and fermentation, another transformation is unfolding—not in laboratories or aging rooms, but in the soil itself.

The Return of American-Grown Tobacco: Rediscovering a Lost Heritage

In the rolling hills of Kentucky and the fertile valleys of Connecticut, a quiet revolution has been taking root. American tobacco, once forgotten in the shadow of Caribbean giants, is reclaiming its place in the global cigar landscape.

The story is more than an agricultural comeback. It is a cultural redemption. For decades, American tobacco was treated as a secondary product, overshadowed by the mythic status of Cuban, Nicaraguan, and Dominican leaves. Now, a new generation of farmers and blenders sees something different—a forgotten heritage waiting to be reimagined.

While fire-cured tobacco has long been used in machine-made cigars and pipe tobacco, its integration into premium handmade cigars represents a new frontier for blending innovation. Drew Estate's Kentucky Fire Cured line, released in 2014, was the first major premium cigar to feature this domestic technique, and other brands, including Antebellum, have followed in exploring fire-cured Kentucky leaf as a premium cigar ingredient. The fire-curing process—an old American technique that involves slow smoking the leaves over hardwood fires—creates a unique flavor profile that challenges everything cigar enthusiasts thought they knew about tobacco.

The potential is more than nostalgic. Innovative blenders now see American tobacco not as a limitation, but as a unique opportunity. The terroir of American tobacco regions—with their distinct soil compositions, microclimates, and agricultural traditions—is offering flavor profiles that cannot be replicated anywhere else in the world.

In Connecticut, small farms in the Connecticut River Valley, continue to cultivate Connecticut Shade and Connecticut Broadleaf tobacco, known for its silky texture and rich flavor.

These farms are not aiming to replicate Cuban or Nicaraguan styles but are instead experimenting with hybrid strains, organic growing methods, and alternative curing techniques, redefining what American-grown premium cigar tobacco can be.

Industry veterans who once dismissed American-grown tobacco are now taking notice. The same spirit of innovation that reshaped other areas of the cigar world is now focused on domestic agriculture. What was once seen as a weakness—the lack of a centuries-old tobacco tradition—is now an advantage. Free from rigid expectations, American blenders can experiment in ways more traditional markets cannot match.

The revival is about more than agriculture. It is a statement of cultural identity. In an era of global markets and international competition, American-grown tobacco represents something powerful—a return to local production, a celebration of domestic craftsmanship.

Some industry insiders are now whispering a radical possibility: What if American cigars could one day rival—or even surpass—their Caribbean counterparts? It is a dream that would have seemed impossible just a decade ago. But in the world of cigar innovation, the impossible is becoming routine.

As American-grown tobacco reclaims its place in the industry, it is becoming part of a broader movement redefining cigar blending itself. The boundaries between tradition and experimentation are dissolving, with master blenders treating each cigar as both an artistic and scientific endeavor.

With American-grown tobacco reentering the premium cigar market, blenders are exploring how its distinct terroir influences modern cigar craftsmanship. Each leaf—whether a silky Connecticut Shade wrapper or a fire-cured Kentucky filler—is no longer just a regional specialty but a vital part of a new generation's blending experiments.

Some of the most innovative work is happening at the margins of traditional production. Small boutique manufacturers, unburdened by the constraints of large-scale production, are the true innovators. They treat each cigar as a unique artistic statement, experimenting with techniques that larger manufacturers would have considered too risky.

The most groundbreaking developments go beyond flavor; they redefine what a cigar can be. Some blenders are incorporating techniques from wine and spirits production, understanding tobacco as a living, evolving product. Terroir has become as important in cigars as it has long been in wine, with specific micro-regions celebrated for their unique characteristics.

Rather than merely adapting to challenges, the industry is entering a new era of reinvention. Cigars are evolving into more than luxury products— they are reflections of terroir, innovation, and the artistry of those redefining what premium tobacco can be.

Technology & The Digital Age: Reimagining Cigar Culture

Once solely defined by heritage and ritual, cigar culture is now at the crossroads of tradition and innovation. The rise of digital tools, artificial intelligence, and blockchain technology is reshaping how cigars are stored, authenticated, and appreciated—bridging the gap between old-world craftsmanship and 21st-century connectivity.

Far from replacing the tactile, sensory experience of cigars, these advancements are enhancing it. Whether through smart humidors that ensure perfect aging conditions, QR-coded provenance tracking to combat counterfeits, or global virtual tastings that connect enthusiasts across continents, technology is revolutionizing the way cigars are enjoyed, discussed, and preserved.

The smart humidor represents a revolution in preservation. Gone are the days of relying on intuition and inherited wisdom. Now, artificial intelligence can analyze humidity, temperature, and aging conditions with scientific precision. These aren't just storage devices; they are time machines that can predict the optimal moment to enjoy a carefully aged cigar.

Blockchain technology has emerged as the unexpected guardian of cigar authenticity. In an era plagued by counterfeit products, luxury brands like Cohiba and Davidoff have found an unlikely ally in digital verification. A simple QR code can now tell the entire story of a cigar—its origin, its journey, its carefully documented provenance. What once required expert knowledge can now be accessed by any smartphone-wielding enthusiast.

Some saw these technological interventions as a threat to traditional cigar culture. But the most innovative enthusiasts understand something profound: technology isn't replacing tradition—it is expanding it. These digital tools are creating new ways of experiencing an ancient craft, making the world of premium cigars more accessible than ever before.

Virtual herfs hosted on Zoom are bringing together enthusiasts from continents apart, creating a democratized space where knowledge is shared freely. Facebook groups have become digital humidors of collective wisdom, where a novice smoker can learn from decades of accumulated expertise. Machine learning is beginning to personalize the cigar experience in ways that would have seemed like science fiction a generation earlier. Artificial intelligence can now recommend cigars based on a smoker's past preferences, creating a kind of digital sommelier that understands individual taste with uncanny precision.

Yet, the most profound transformation isn't technological—it is cultural. These digital communities are preserving and expanding cigar culture, not replacing it. They are creating a global dialogue that celebrates craftsmanship, shares stories, and connects enthusiasts in ways no physical lounge ever could.

What has emerged is more than a digital trend. It is a new way of experiencing an ancient tradition—a bridge between old-world craftsmanship and 21st-century connectivity. The cigar is no longer just a product. It is a global conversation, waiting to be explored.

WHAT WILL THEY SMOKE?

The Future of Cigar Consumption

The crystal ball of cigar consumption reveals a landscape both familiar and radically transformed. The smokers of tomorrow will not simply consume cigars—they will curate experiences, collect stories, and engage with tobacco in ways that challenge every traditional notion of consumption.

The Next Generation of Collectors

Young enthusiasts are reimagining cigars as more than just a smoking experience. They are treating them as cultural artifacts, investment vehicles, and statements of personal identity. Where previous generations collected stamps or wines, millennials and Gen Z are building carefully curated cigar collections that tell complex personal narratives.

Technology will play a crucial role. Blockchain-verified rare cigars, AI-powered aging recommendations, and digital provenance tracking will transform collecting from a passive hobby to an active, data-driven pursuit. A limited edition cigar won't just be a smoke—it will be a digital asset with a complete, transparent history.

Sustainability and Ethical Consumption

Future smokers will demand more than quality. They will want transparency about tobacco sourcing, environmental impact, and the social conditions of tobacco farmers. Boutique brands that can tell a compelling story of sustainable production will command premium prices and loyalty.

Hybrid Experiences

Cigar appreciation is evolving beyond traditional settings. Digital platforms will continue to shape the way enthusiasts explore new blends, engage in expert-led tastings, and build collections—merging tradition with technology.

Micro-Production and Hyper-Personalization

In addition to boutique brands, cigars may belong as much to ultra-small batch producers who can offer completely personalized experiences. Imagine cigars blended specifically for an individual's palate, with genetic flavor profile matching and custom aging processes.

The Ritual Reimagined

For the next generation, smoking a cigar will transcend mere consumption, evolving into an act of connection—a deeper connection to tradition, to global communities, and to the intricate stories of agriculture and craftsmanship. The cigar will become a medium for storytelling, a bridge between past and future.

In this new world, the question won't be simply "What will they smoke?" but "What will they smoke—and what story will they tell?"

The Crossroads of Tradition and Innovation

In the soft glow of a cigar lounge, between wisps of carefully cultivated smoke, the future of cigars is being quietly reimagined. This is not an ending, but a transformation.

The cigar industry stands on the cusp of extraordinary potential. Regulatory challenges that once seemed insurmountable are now catalyzing innovation. New global markets in China, India, and the Middle East are expanding the very definition of cigar culture. Digital technologies are creating connections that would have been unimaginable to previous generations of tobacco craftsmen.

What remains constant is the core essence of the cigar—a testament to patience, craftsmanship, and human connection. From the fields where tobacco is grown to the hands that roll each leaf, from the collectors who preserve rare blends to the communities that share their passion online, cigars continue to be more than a product. They are a living narrative of human creativity.

The next chapter of this story will be written not by governments or corporations, but by the passionate individuals who see beyond current limitations. The young blenders experimenting with hybrid tobacco strains, the digital collectors tracking rare cigars through blockchain, the enthusiasts creating global communities—they are the true architects of the cigar's future.

Tradition and innovation are not opposing forces. They are partners in an ongoing conversation. As they have for over 250 years, cigars will continue to adapt and surprise.

The future of cigars is unwritten. And that is its greatest promise.

"I have made it a rule never to smoke more than one cigar at a time."

— MARK TWAIN

———

Twain meant it as a joke about moderation. But two and a half centuries after Israel Putnam carried his donkey loads of Cuban cigars back to Connecticut, the line lands differently. The American cigar story is, in the end, a story about deliberate enjoyment: the patience to do one thing slowly, well, and on purpose, in a country that has rarely valued any of those things.

CONCLUSION

A Legacy of Smoke & Craftsmanship

For more than 250 years, cigars have been an integral part of American history | Cigars have been present in moments of war and peace, prosperity and hardship, revolution and industry. Cigars have symbolized power, craftsmanship, and social connection—shared by presidents and soldiers, industrial titans and working-class laborers alike.

Despite economic upheavals, government restrictions, and shifting cultural attitudes, cigars have endured. They have outlasted prohibitionist movements, survived embargos, and adapted to global market transformations. And today, in an increasingly fast-paced, digital world, the ritual of the cigar—its slow, deliberate burn—remains a quiet act of defiance.

The Cigar's Journey Through American History

In this book, we have traced the evolution of cigars through pivotal moments in American history:

- From Colonial Roots to Industrial Dominance – The early American tobacco trade, the rise of cigar factories, and the golden age of American cigar manufacturing.
- The War Years and Political Influence – Cigars as a battlefield comfort, a tool of diplomacy, and a fixture in the backrooms of power.

- The Cuban Embargo and Industry Reinvention – How the 1962 ban on Cuban imports forced cigar makers to adapt, shifting production to new regions and reshaping the global tobacco trade.
- The Rise, Fall, and Revival of the American Cigar Industry – From the near-collapse of domestic production in the late 20th century to the boutique renaissance that revitalized the craft.
- The Modern Cigar at a Crossroads — How regulation, globalization, and a new generation of consumers are reshaping the industry today.

As cigar culture evolved, its transformation did not stop with geography and exclusivity. The forces of technology, social media, and shifting consumer habits have accelerated this change, redefining how cigars are enjoyed, discussed, and shared.

The Reimagining of the Cigar Culture

What we have traced across these pages is not the story of an industry frozen in time, but of one continually reinvented by the people who carry it forward. The cigar that Israel Putnam carried home from Cuba in 1762 and the cigar passed around a Discord channel in 2025 are, in some real sense, the same object — yet the world built around it has been remade many times over.

Each generation has had to answer the same question in different terms: what is a cigar *for*? For colonial merchants, it was a quiet declaration of independence from British smoking habits. For Civil War officers, it was comfort and rank. For Gilded Age titans, it was a credential. For exiled Cuban masters in the 1960s, it was the survival of a craft. For the boutique generation, it has been a return to slowness in an accelerating world.

That this question keeps getting asked — and answered, and asked again — is itself the answer. A product that endures for 250 years across war, revolution, regulation, and reinvention is not a relic. It is a tradition that has chosen to stay alive by changing.

The future will keep posing the question. And the cigar is already answering, increasingly, in voices the industry never used to hear: a younger, more diverse, more globally connected generation of smokers and makers who are claiming a tradition older than themselves and choosing to carry it forward.

Final Reflections: Why Cigars Will Always Endure

Unlike mass-market cigarettes, cigars are not merely a habit—they are an experience. In a world of instant gratification, the ritual of a slow-burning cigar is a quiet rebellion against the fast pace of modern life. It demands presence, appreciation, and patience—qualities increasingly rare in an era dominated by quick consumption.

As long as there are those who value craftsmanship, tradition, and the artistry of a finely rolled cigar, the legacy will endure—one smoke at a time.

Preserve the culture. Pass down its stories. Honor its traditions.

A cigar is history, held between your fingers. And perhaps, as you read this, you held one too.

This is America's cigar story—a legacy that burns on.

Endnotes

Chapter 1: The Foundations of American Cigar Culture

1. New Orleans was a center of cigar manufacturing in the 19th century, with Cuban cigar makers relocating there (along with Key West and New York) after the 1857 U.S. tariff disrupted the Cuban export trade. The Gulf trade route connecting New Orleans to Tampico, Veracruz, and Havana supplied raw tobacco from both Cuba and the San Andrés Tuxtla tobacco-growing region of Veracruz. San Francisco emerged as the West Coast's cigar manufacturing and distribution hub in the same period, though its industry was driven primarily by direct East Coast trade (via the Panama route and, after 1869, the Transcontinental Railroad) and by a substantial local Chinese-immigrant cigar-making workforce, rather than by Pacific routes through Mexico.

Chapter 3: The Rise of the American Cigar Industry

2. In 1900, the distinction between machine-made and hand-rolled cigars was not yet fully established in the market. Premium hand-rolled domestic cigars typically sold for 10–25 cents, with top-tier imported Havanas commanding 25 cents to $1.00 or more. Workingman's cigars—sometimes called 'two-fers' or 'nickel cigars'—anchored the popular market at 5–10 cents and were produced using a mix of traditional hand-rolling and early mechanization. Consumers at the time primarily associated price with quality rather than production method. The clear market segmentation between machine-made and hand-rolled cigars did not emerge until the widespread adoption of fully automated cigar rolling machines in the 1920s and 1930s, when brands like Cremo built entire ad campaigns attacking machine-made competitors as inferior.

Appendix A

The Narrative of Cigar Advertising in America

Cigar advertising has always been a reflection of American culture, evolving alongside economic shifts, regulations, and technology. From handbills in the 19th century to social media campaigns today, marketing has shaped how cigars are perceived—not just as tobacco products, but as symbols of success, craftsmanship, and tradition.

Early Advertising (1800s–1900s): Storytelling & National Identity

Early cigar ads emphasized craftsmanship, national pride, and aspiration. Brands romanticized tobacco cultivation, factory labor, and cigar-smoking as a mark of success. Figures like businessmen and politicians were often featured to reinforce cigars as symbols of power and refinement.

The Golden Age (1920s–1950s): Lifestyle & Status

Marketing evolved from simple product promotion to lifestyle branding. Cigars became associated with masculinity, achievement, and social prestige.

Notable Campaigns:

- King Edward Cigars (1930s) – Positioned as refined yet accessible.
- White Owl (1940s–1950s) – Marketed to middle-class workers and WWII veterans.
- Dutch Masters (1950s–1960s) – Linked cigars to cultural refinement using classical art themes.

Regulations & Industry Adaptation (1960s–1990s)

- The 1965 Federal Cigarette Labeling and Advertising Act and the 1969 Public Health Cigarette Smoking Act (which banned cigarette advertising on radio and television beginning in 1971) restricted cigarette marketing, indirectly impacting cigars by tightening the cultural climate around all tobacco advertising.
- The 1998 Master Settlement Agreement, while focused on cigarette manufacturers, reshaped the broader tobacco marketing landscape and accelerated the cigar industry's shift toward niche, luxury-focused branding.
- Cigar advertising moved into magazines, private clubs, and word-of-mouth promotion.

The Cigar Boom & Digital Age (1990s–Present)

The 1990s saw a resurgence in cigar culture, fueled by *Cigar Aficionado* and celebrity endorsements. As regulations tightened, brands turned to digital marketing, influencer partnerships, and online communities.

Modern Trends:

- Social Media & Influencer Marketing – Cigar reviewers and Instagram personalities now drive brand awareness.
- Blockchain Authentication – Used to combat counterfeits and enhance brand exclusivity.
- Limited Edition Releases – Create hype similar to luxury sneakers and craft whiskey drops.

Conclusion: The Future of Cigar Marketing

Cigar advertising has shifted from print to digital, from mass appeal to exclusive branding and storytelling. The future lies in tech-driven authenticity, sustainability, and global engagement, ensuring cigars remain a luxury experience, deeply rooted in tradition yet adaptable to modern consumer expectations.

Appendix B

Labor Movements & Union Agreements in the Cigar Industry

Introduction: The Human Story Behind the Smoke

The cigar industry is more than a tale of tobacco and trade—it's a profound narrative of human struggle, resilience, and collective action. From tenement workshops to factory floors, cigar workers shaped not just an industry, but the broader landscape of American labor rights.

Quantitative Context:

• Peak Union Membership: 45,000 cigar workers (1920s)
• Average Weekly Wage: $11.50 in 1900 (compared to $8.75 in other manufacturing)
• Ethnic Composition: 62% immigrant workers (primarily Cuban, Spanish, and Italian)
• Current Union Representation: Less than 8% of original peak membership (2025)

Early Labor Movements: The Foundations of Resistance

Key Pioneering Organizations:

Cigar Makers' International Union (CMIU) — Founded 1864 in New York City as the Cigar Makers National Union (became 'International' in 1867 after Canadian locals affiliated). Samuel Gompers, himself a cigarmaker, rose to prominence within the CMIU in the 1870s and went on to found the American Federation of Labor in 1886

Working Conditions Pre-Unionization:

• 12-16 hour workdays
• Piecework compensation
• Minimal workplace safety regulations
• High rates of respiratory diseases
• Child labor prevalent

Landmark Strikes and Transformative Moments

1. Tampa Cigar Strikes (1910s-1930s)
   • Epicenter: Ybor City, Florida
   • Key Participants: Cuban, Spanish, and Italian workers
   • Primary Demands:
     o Wage increases
     o Improved factory conditions
     o Protection against mechanization
       • Impact: Established blueprint for industrial labor organizing
2. Charleston Cigar Strike (1945-1946)
   • Pioneering African American Labor Action
   • Led primarily by women workers
   • Challenged racial discrimination

- Confronted American Tobacco Company
- Duration: Six months
- Outcome: Modest wage increases, significant symbolic victory
- Cultural legacy: The Charleston picket line is where striking workers, led by Lucille Simmons, first sang 'We Will Overcome,' adapted from a gospel hymn. The song would later become 'We Shall Overcome,' the defining anthem of the civil rights movement.

Union Agreements: Reshaping Industrial Relations

Critical Contractual Milestones:

- 1921 CMIU Agreement: First comprehensive industry-wide wage standard
- 1947 Taft-Hartley Act: Complicated but ultimately reinforced collective bargaining
- 1960s Decline: Offshoring and mechanization weakened union powe

Modern Labor Landscape

Contemporary Challenges:
- Globalization of cigar production
- Shift to overseas manufacturing
- Automation of rolling processes
- Reduced union membership

Current State of Cigar Labor:
- Estimated 3,000 union workers remaining (2025)
- Boutique brands emphasizing artisanal craftsmanship
- Growing interest in worker conditions and fair trade practices

Technological and Cultural Shifts:
- Digital platforms monitoring workplace conditions
- Increased transparency in production methods
- Rising consumer awareness about labor practices

Emerging Trends:
- Rise of worker-owned cooperatives in boutique cigar production
- Increased focus on sustainable and ethical labor practices
- Growing interest in documenting and preserving artisanal rolling techniques
- Digital platforms creating new forms of worker solidarity and skill sharing

Conclusion: The Enduring Legacy

The story of cigar industry labor is a testament to worker resilience. From tenement workshops to global production lines, these workers transformed not just an industry, but the very concept of labor rights in America. Their struggles continue to inspire modern labor movements, reminding us that every cigar carries within it a narrative of human determination and the ongoing quest for dignity in work.

Appendix C

Notable Cigar Brands & Their Histories

Introduction: Crafting Legacy, One Leaf at a Time

The story of American cigars is written not just in tobacco leaves, but in the narratives of the brands that have shaped, transformed, and revolutionized the industry. This appendix explores the most influential cigar brands, tracing their evolution from small family operations to global icons.

Tier 1: Legacy Brands - The Pioneers
1. J.C. Newman (1895 - Present)
    • Oldest Family-Owned Cigar Company in the U.S.
    • Market Position: Produces both premium handmade and machine-made cigars.
2. Arturo Fuente (1912 - Present)
    • Founded in West Tampa, Florida
    • Current Valuation: Privately held; specific financials undisclosed.
    • Legendary Line: OpusX - considered the first true Dominican puro

Tier 2: Disruptive Innovators
3. Drew Estate (1996 - Present)
    • Revolutionized cigar marketing
    • Breakthrough Product: ACID infused cigars. Liga Privada line established Drew Estate as a serious player in the premium cigar market
    • Current Ownership: Acquired by Swisher International in 2014
4. Padron (1964 - Present)
    • Nicaraguan Tobacco Specialists
    • Signature Series: 1964 Anniversary Edition
    • Industry Impact: Elevated Nicaraguan tobacco's global reputation

Tier 3: Emerging Brands - The New Wave
5. Warped Cigars (2007 - Present)
    • Boutique brand focusing on small-batch production
    • Specialty: Cuban-inspired blending techniques
    • Market Positioning: High-end, collector-focused releases
6. Antebellum (Launched in 2025)
    • Newest entrant in American-grown tobacco movement
    • Unique Selling Proposition: Exclusively multi-region U.S. tobacco blends
    • Regions Utilized: Kentucky, Pennsylvania, Connecticut, and beyond
    • Innovative Project: Blends inspired by history and heritage
7. Foundation Cigars (2015 - Present)
    • Boutique cigar brand. Founded by master blender Nicholas Melillo, formerly Drew Estate's Executive VP of International Operations.
    • Critically acclaimed with multiple top cigar ratings

- Known for innovative blending techniques
- Represents the craft and storytelling approach to modern cigar production

Additional Insights:

Market Dynamics: The global cigar industry is dominated by major players like Imperial Brands' subsidiary Altadis and the Scandinavian Tobacco Group.

Emerging Trends: Brands like Antebellum are part of a growing movement focusing on American-grown tobaccos, reflecting a resurgence in domestic cigar craftsmanship.

Digital Age Transformation

Modern Cigar Brand Characteristics:
- Blockchain authentication
- Limited edition releases
- Direct-to-consumer marketing
- Influencer collaborations
- Storytelling-driven branding

Global Cigar Market (2025)
- Market Size: $24.27 billion globally
- U.S. Market Share: Approximately 30%
- Growth Rate: Approximately 5% CAGR (boutique and craft cigars often exceed this growth rate due to premiumization trends)
- Growth Sectors: Boutique and craft premium cigars
- Emerging Markets: Asia and Eastern Europe

Technological Integration
- QR code tracking
- Augmented reality packaging[17]
- Sustainability certifications
- Craft production transparency

Conclusion: Beyond Tobacco

These brands represent more than commercial entities. They are storytellers, cultural ambassadors, and guardians of a craft that spans centuries. From family workshops to global enterprises, they continue to write the evolving narrative of American cigars.

---

[17] Augmented Reality (AR) Packaging: Technology allowing smartphone-based interactive experiences with product packaging.

Appendix D

Timeline of Major Events in U.S. Cigar History

The American Cigar Journey: A Chronological Exploration

Pre-Industrial Era (1600s-1800s)
• 1612: John Rolfe successfully cultivates tobacco in Jamestown, Virginia
• 1762: First commercial cigar production in the United States
• 1840: Cuban cigar imports surge, becoming a luxury staple in American port cities
• 1864: Cigar Makers' International Union founded

Industrial Revolution & Golden Age (1870-1920)
• 1880s-1920s: Hand-rolled cigar production dominates the U.S. tobacco industry, peaking in the late 1920s before mechanization and the Depression caused decline
• 1900s: Tampa earns the title "Cigar Capital of the World"
• 1905: Over 4 billion cigars produced annually
• 1920s: Peak of Cuban tobacco imports

Regulatory & Economic Transformations (1920-1960)
• 1933: End of Prohibition revives bar, restaurant, and social-club culture where cigar consumption thrived
• 1880s-1920s: Cigar-rolling machines spread, gradually displacing hand-rolling for inexpensive cigar lines
• 1962: Cuban Trade Embargo implemented
• 1964: Pre-modern peak of U.S. cigar consumption (~9 billion units, coinciding with the Surgeon General's report)

Modern Era Milestones (1960-2025)
• 1965: First tobacco advertising restrictions
• 1992: Cigar Aficionado magazine launches
• 1994: Premium cigar boom begins
• 2016: FDA attempts to regulate premium cigars
• 2021: COVID-19 pandemic impacts global cigar production
• 2025: Emergence of Antebellum, highlighting American-grown tobacco renaissance

Technological & Cultural Shifts
• Late 1990s: Cigar-related websites and online retail begin to emerge
• 2010: Social media transforms cigar culture
• 2020: Blockchain authentication introduced
• 2025: AI-driven blending and marketing techniques emerge

- 1960: Cuban embargo disrupts global tobacco trade
- 1990: Dominican Republic becomes leading cigar exporter
- 2010: Nicaraguan cigars gain international recognition
- 2025: Emerging markets in Asia and Eastern Europe

Regulatory Landscape Evolution
- 1965: First federal tobacco advertising restrictions
- 1998: Master Settlement Agreement
- 2009: FDA gains tobacco regulation authority
- 2016: Proposed FDA premium cigar regulations
- 2025: FDA denied authority to regulate premium cigar
- 2025: Increased focus on sustainability and ethical production

Conclusion: A Living History

This timeline is more than a chronology—it's a testament to the resilience, innovation, and cultural significance of the American cigar industry. From colonial plantations to global digital marketplaces, the story continues to unfold.

Bibliography

Chapter 1: The Foundations of American Cigar Culture

Primary Sources and Memoirs

- Grant, Ulysses S. *Personal Memoirs of U.S. Grant*. New York: Charles L. Webster & Co., 1885.
- Twain, Mark. *Roughing It*. Hartford, CT: American Publishing Company, 1872.
- Roosevelt, Theodore. *Theodore Roosevelt: An Autobiography*. New York: Macmillan, 1913.

Historical and Government Archives

- United States Census Bureau. *Manufactures of Tobacco: Bulletin on Manufactures*, 1900. Washington, D.C.: Government Printing Office.
- University of Maryland Libraries. *Cigar Makers' International Union of America Records, 0097-LBR*. Special Collections and University Archives, College Park, MD.

Academic Books and Journal Articles

- Gately, Iain. *Tobacco: A Cultural History of How an Exotic Plant Seduced Civilization*. New York: Grove Press, 2001.
- Goodman, Jordan. *Tobacco in History: The Cultures of Dependence*. London: Routledge, 1993.
- University Press, 1987.

Archival Materials

- Cuban Heritage Collection. University of Miami.

Chapter 2: The Rise of the American Cigar Industry

Primary and Archival Sources

- Grant, Ulysses S. *Personal Memoirs of U.S. Grant*. New York: Charles L. Webster & Co., 1885.
- United States Census Bureau. *Manufactures of Tobacco: Bulletin on Manufactures*. Washington, D.C.: Government Printing Office, 1900.
- University of Maryland Libraries. *Cigar Makers' International Union of America Records, 0097-LBR*. Special Collections and University Archives, College Park, MD.

Academic Books and Dissertations

- Gately, Iain. *Tobacco: A Cultural History of How an Exotic Plant Seduced Civilization*. New York: Grove Press, 2001.

- Goodman, Jordan. *Tobacco in History: The Cultures of Dependence*. London: Routledge, 1993.
- Kluger, Richard. *Ashes to Ashes: America's Hundred-Year Cigarette War*. New York: Knopf, 1996.
- Porter, Glenn. *The Rise of Big Business, 1860–1920*. Arlington Heights, IL: Harlan Davidson, 2006.

Archival Archives

- Cuban Heritage Collection, University of Miami.

Chapter 3: Smoke-Filled Rooms & The Politics of Power

Personal Papers and Memoirs

- Grant, Ulysses S. *Personal Memoirs of U.S. Grant*. New York: Charles L. Webster & Co., 1885.
- Roosevelt, Theodore. *Theodore Roosevelt: An Autobiography*. New York: Macmillan, 1913.
- Salinger, Pierre. *With Kennedy*. Garden City, NY: Doubleday, 1966.

Government Records and Political History

- United States. *Presidential Proclamation 3447*. Federal Register, February 7, 1962.
- United States Department of State. *Foreign Relations of the United States, 1961–1963, Volume X: Cuba*. Washington, D.C.: U.S. Government Printing Office, 1997.

Historical and Academic Books

- Gately, Iain. *Tobacco: A Cultural History of How an Exotic Plant Seduced Civilization*. New York: Grove Press, 2001.
- Goodman, Jordan. *Tobacco in History: The Cultures of Dependence*. London: Routledge, 1993.
- Kluger, Richard. *Ashes to Ashes: America's Hundred-Year Cigarette War*. New York: Knopf, 1996.
- Porter, Glenn. *The Rise of Big Business, 1860–1920*. Arlington Heights, IL: Harlan Davidson, 2006.
- Sennett, Richard. *The Fall of Public Man*. New York: W.W. Norton, 1992.

Archival and Club Resources

- University of Maryland Libraries. *Cigar Makers' International Union of America Records, 0097-LBR*.
- Cuban Heritage Collection, University of Miami.

Chapter 4: The Cuban Embargo – A Defining Disruption

Primary and Government Sources
- United States. *Presidential Proclamation 3447*. *Federal Register*, February 7, 1962.
- United States Department of State. *Foreign Relations of the United States, 1961–1963, Volume X: Cuba*. Washington, D.C.: U.S. Government Printing Office, 1997.
- Economic Research Service. *Cuba Shifts Trade in Farm Products to Soviet Bloc*. March 7, 1962.
- Radelat, Andrea. "From Revenge to Reconciliation with Cuba." *CT Mirror*, December 19, 2014.

Memoirs and Interviews
- Salinger, Pierre. *With Kennedy*. Garden City, NY: Doubleday, 1966.

Historical and Academic Books
- Gately, Iain. *Tobacco: A Cultural History of How an Exotic Plant Seduced Civilization*. New York: Grove Press, 2001.

Archival Sources
- Cuban Heritage Collection, University of Miami.

Chapter 5: The 1990s Cigar Revival

Media and Cultural Studies
- Mass Affluence." *Journal of Consumer Culture* 14, no. 3 (2017): 451–469.

Historical and Archival Sources
- Font, Mauricio A., and Alfonso W. Quiroz, eds. *The Cuban Republic and José Martí: Reception and Use of a National Symbol*. Lanham: Lexington Books, 2006.

Archival Sources
- Cuban Heritage Collection, University of Miami

Chapter 6: The Boutique Cigar Renaissance

Industry Studies and Contemporary Market Research
- **Cigar Association of America.** "Cigar Imports 2024: Premiums Steady, Total Volume Eases." Cigar Association of America, 2025. https://cigarsusa.org/cigar-imports-2024-premiums-steady-total-volume-eases/

Books and Monographs
- Gately, Iain. *Tobacco: A Cultural History of How an Exotic Plant Seduced Civilization*. New York: Grove Press, 2001.
- Kluger, Richard. *Ashes to Ashes: America's Hundred-Year Cigarette War*. New York: Knopf, 1996.

Chapter 7: The Future of the Cigar Industry

Government Reports and Regulatory Sources

- *Cigar Association of America v. FDA*, U.S. Court of Appeals for the D.C. Circuit, No. 23-5220 (D.C. Cir. Jan. 24, 2025).
- U.S. Food and Drug Administration. "Deeming Tobacco Products To Be Subject to the Federal Food, Drug, and Cosmetic Act, as Amended by the Family Smoking Prevention and Tobacco Control Act; Restrictions on the Sale and Distribution of Tobacco Products and Required Warning Statements for Tobacco Products." Final Rule. *Federal Register* 81, no. 90 (May 10, 2016): 28973–29106. To be codified at 21 C.F.R. pts. 1100, 1140, and 1143.
- United States. *Presidential Proclamation 3447*. *Federal Register*, February 7, 1962.
- United States Department of State. *Foreign Relations of the United States, 1961–1963, Volume X: Cuba*. Washington, D.C.: Government Printing Office, 1997.

Historical and Cultural Context

- Gately, Iain. *Tobacco: A Cultural History of How an Exotic Plant Seduced Civilization*. New York: Grove Press, 2001.
- Kluger, Richard. *Ashes to Ashes: America's Hundred-Year Cigarette War*. New York: Knopf, 1996.

Index

A

B

C

Q

R

S

T

U

About the Author

Sebastian Saviano is a writer and researcher whose work explores American craft, ritual, and identity. He is the author of *America's Cigar Story: The History, Politics, and Legacy of Cigars from 1762 to the Modern Era*, the first volume of *The American Cigar Series*. The next volume, *Smoke & Oak: The Shared Legacy of Bourbon and Cigars*, continues the story by tracing how America's two great native crafts grew up alongside each other.

Trained in political theory at Georgetown University, he writes about the cultural lives of the things Americans make, drink, and pass around the table — and what those things have to say about who we are.

About *The American Cigar Series*

Volume 1 — *America's Cigar Story: The History, Politics, and Legacy of Cigars from 1762 to the Modern Era* *(this volume)* The foundational volume of the series. From colonial Virginia tobacco fields through Civil War generals, postwar prosperity, and the boutique revival, *America's Cigar Story* traces how a hand-rolled product became a fixture of American economic, political, and cultural life.

Volume 2 — *Smoke & Oak: The Shared Legacy of Bourbon and Cigars* (2025) A parallel history of America's two great native crafts. Bourbon and cigars rose together, struggled through the same wars and embargoes, weathered the same regulatory battles, and found their renaissance in the same lounges and back rooms. *Smoke & Oak* explores why they belong together — in the glass, in the hand, and in the American imagination.

Volume 3 — *The American Puro: The All-American Cigar's Forgotten History* *(forthcoming)* The story of cigars made entirely from U.S.-grown tobacco — a tradition older than most readers realize, and one being quietly revived by a new generation of American growers and rollers.

Volume 4 — *Cigar America: Tobacco, Masculinity, and the Myth of Power* *(forthcoming)* A cultural essay on how the cigar became shorthand for power, defiance, and American masculinity — from Grant's stogie to Castro's Cohiba, from boardroom rituals to Tony Montana's final scene. What remains, the book asks, when the smoke clears?

.

www.ingramcontent.com/pod-product-compliance
Lightning Source LLC
Chambersburg PA
CBHW051619120626
46551CB00014B/1863